Metropolitan Police Divers

Log Book

Underwater Search Unit
1984 to 1988

ACTUAL LOG BOOK OF

MACKENZIE WILLIAM MOULTON

Who served with the London Police diving unit for 13 years of his 30 year service.

Front Cover

POLICE DIVERS LOG BOOK

www.mackenzie-moultonartist.pixels.com

1983 The Beginning

About November 1983, applications were put out on Thames Division, the marine side of the Metropolitan Police, for volunteers to apply for posts as divers in the Underwater Search Unit. This appealed to me, as I had spent a lot of time diving in Malta and the thought of doing something I enjoyed in my leisure time and being paid for it seemed too good to be true.

Before being selected for the Underwater Search Unit all applicants had to undergo a few tests. One of the tests was to swim 20 lengths of a standard size swimming pool, then do the same with a weight belt and snorkel. Each applicant was then taught basic lifeline signals and how the self-contained breathing apparatus (scuba) worked. Once we were happy with the scuba, we were in turn put under the water in a blacked out mask, this was to see if anyone suffered from claustrophobia.

After all these tests were successfully carried out to the satisfaction of the Underwater Search Unit Inspector, it was then up to one's performance at an interview in front of Senior Officers of Thames Division, including the Inspector in charge of the USU, who would question the candidates as to their suitability. Most of the questions were about diving, for example, how do you feel about going underwater in nil visibility, and finding a dead body; do you understand the risk involved; what does your wife think of it; are you prepared to be on 24 hour call, and turn out at any time night or day whatever the weather.

The only unusual question I remember quite clearly was put to me by the Inspector in charge of the USU who said, 'Are you prepared to take your turn in cleaning out the porta loo on the USU lorry?' Well, I thought, of course, the unit spends 50% of it's time diving in shit anyway, so what's the big deal about cleaning the porta loo.

When the final choice was made I came second, and the reason given to me was the man that was chosen above me had previously been a Port of London diver and already held a commercial diver's certificate, and it was thought he would be more likely to pass the 8 week course at the National Police Diver Training School.

My heart sank and I thought my chance had gone. I was already 36 years old, and that was considered the maximum age for entry into the unit.

The diving unit was a very small team of men out of thirty thousand members of The Metropolitan Police Force. Entry was mostly filling dead men's shoes.

By the time there was going to be another vacancy I would be too old.

Fortunately for me the preferred candidate failed his medical and I was next in line for the vacancy.

I have already written a book on the Metropolitan Police Underwater Search Unit, but thought it would be nice to record my log books before all the stories and information are lost in time, so basically I have copied every page of the log book for you to read as it is.

We were told not only to record our police diving but leisure diving as well, so you will see records of dives I have done as an Advanced BSAC diver.

There are several abbreviation you may not be familiar with like, nil viz, which means you cant see you hand in front of your face, and Aga used, that's a positive pressure full face mask diving valve made by a company called AGA. Pos, is another full face mask we use, made by a company called Poseidon, but unlike the AGA which is positive pressure its an on demand regulator. Stby means standby diver who is always dressed ready to come to your assistance if you get trapped, and the numbers relate to each police officer. Attds means divers attendants, when not diving you become a divers attendant, making sure they are dressed correctly, equipment is tested and taking care of their life line.

Sup indicates the officer allocated to supervise the dive

I hope you enjoy this unusual book.   Mackenzie

Self Portrait of the Author, now on permanent display in
the Thames Police Association Museum, London

PAINTING OF THE MET POLICE UNDERWATER
SEARCH UNIT IN VICTORIA DOCK

From left, Mackenzie Moulton (Author and artist) James
Holgate (Divers handler} John Newson (Diver in the
water) John Smith (Standby divers handler) John Hughs
(Standby Diver)

Officer nominated as Diving Contractor ....

FOREWORD

This Log Book is issued in accordance with the Health and Safety Diving Operations at Work Regulations, 1981, to each member of the Underwater Search Unit. It is a personal log and details are to be entered as soon as possible after each dive.

COMPRESSED AIR DIVING

Operations Column of Log will include:—

1. Type of operation and method used.

2. Breathing apparatus i.e. S.C.U.B.A. or S.D.D.E.

3. Equipment used i.e. specialised equipment.

Remarks Column of Log will include:—

1. Any Decompression Schedule used by the diver.

2. Any Decompression sickness or other illness, discomfort or injury suffered by the diver.

3. Any other factor relevant to his health or safety.

THE LOG WILL BE EXAMINED BY THE OFFICER IN CHARGE MONTHLY

THIS DOCUMENT MUST BE KEPT FOR A MINIMUM PERIOD OF TWO YEARS FROM THE LAST ENTRY

Printed and Published by Lancashire Constabulary, Hutton, Preston.

PERSONAL DETAILS

Surname: .... Moulton ....

Christian Names: .... Mackenzie William ....

Rank and Number: .... P C 224ᵐ ....

Date of Birth: .... 21 - 6 - 1947 ....

Signature of Holder: .... M Moulton ....

Telephone No. Force HQ.: .... 01 - 488 - 5096 ....

Approved Doctor: .... Dr. Minis ....

Telephone No.: ....

① 1984

Date	Location	Details of Operation
18/1/84	Regents Canal near St Pancras Way, Kings X under Road Bridge	Training Dive. One L/S Ladies DLP 735 Cycle Removed. Conveyed to ED where deposited by WPC 990 booking Attends at location PC 110 Brotherton, PC 171 Keal. Stand by PC Lawson SCUBA

TIMES				Max Depth Metres	Remarks	Signatures of (a) Diver (b) Supervisor
Left Surface	Left Bottom	Bottom Time	Reached Surface			
1030		30	1100	2m.	2ft Vis	(a)
						(b)

Date	Location	Details of Operation		

②

Date	Location	Details of Operation
19/1/84	Regent's Canal. at Regent's Canal Dock near Lock Gates near Commercial Road	Training Dive along jack stay. Standby Diver John Hughes. Attendant PC Brotherton & PC Lawson. Insp Johns Supervising SCUBA
③ 24/1/84	WOOLWICH DRY DOCK AQUATIC CENTRE	Training Dive dawn shot Dive Signal Tests SCUBA

TIMES				Max Depth Metres	Remarks	Signatures of (a) Diver (b) Supervisor
Left Surface	Left Bottom	Bottom Time	Reached Surface			
1200		30	1230	2	2ft Vis (a)	
					(b)	
1120		20	1140	10	1ft Vis (a)	
					(b)	

Date	Location	Details of Operation
(4) 26/1/84	YORK WAY N.1. Regents Canal.	Training Dive. Bridge Search and use of Signals · SCUBA
(5) 28-1-84	GRAND UNION CANAL EALING ROAD WEMBLEY	Training Dive life line and Signal excercise Poseidon Equip used. SCUBA
(6) 2/2/84	SERPENTINE. SE CORNER HYDE PARK.	Training Dive. Search and Signal excercise. Pos Equip used SCUBA ·

TIMES				Max Depth Metres	Remarks	Signatures of (a) Diver (b) Supervisor
Left Surface	Left Bottom	Bottom Time	Reached Surface			
1100			1135	2	N.1 vis (a)	
					(b)	P.24
1200			1230	2.1	N.1 vis (a)	
					(b)	
1030			1115.	4.	2ft vic (a)	
					(b)	

Date	Location	Details of Operation
(7) 3/2/84	WOOLWICH. DRY DOCK AQUATIC CENTRE	Training Dive Shot line Jackstay Search Pattern and Signal tests Sup Insp John SCUBA.
(8) 4-2-84	RIVER LEA. LEA BRIDGE ROAD N16	Training Dive in Soft mud Bottom. Nil vis. Search Pattern and signal test. Supervisor John Hughes SCUBA
(9) 6/2/84	KESTON POND.	Training Dive in weed and Lily Pad. SCUBA

TIMES				Max Depth Metres	Remarks	Signatures of (a) Diver (b) Supervisor
Left Surface	Left Bottom	Bottom Time	Reached Surface			
1100			1130	10	4ft Vis (a)	*signature*
					(b)	*signature*
					(a)	*signature*
~~1105~~ 1030			1105	2.1	Nil Vis (b)	*signature*
1202			1244	2.1	4ft Vis (a)	*signature*
					(b)	*signature*

Date	Location	Details of Operation
(10)		
11/2/84	REGENTS CANAL BEN JOHNSON ROAD	Search for white TV. involved in incident (HD dealing) Standby 114. Supv. PS24. P.O.O.S1 used. Attds 167-144. Result No trace. SCUBA
(11) 13/2/84	Girling Reservoir Chingford	Training Dive. P.O.s equip used Wet Hood. Emergency Procedure Supv Insp John. Stilby Jim Hulgate SCUBA
(12) 14/2/84	Millwall Dock. South Section	Training Dive use of AGA / DV & subcom Comms Jump Entry. Supv. John Hughes. Hy Bale Brohat SCUBA

TIMES				Max Depth Metres	Remarks	Signatures of (a) Diver (b) Supervisor
Left Surface	Left Bottom	Bottom Time	Reached Surface			
1150			1230	3	Nil vis (a)	
					(b)	
1115			1200	13	8ft vis (a)	
					(b)	
					(a)	
1050			1120	10	8ft vis	
					(b)	

Date	Location	Details of Operation
(13)		
21/²/84	Gurling Reservion Chingford.	Training Div Signals & Emerg Procedure. Std by 144 AHHs 114-143. Ross / wet hood used. SCUBA
(14)		
5/⁸/84	River Thames. Lower Pool. off M.P. Workshop Dunning.	Training Dive in Tidal Water. Nil Vis. Std by 110 Brotherton SCUBA
(15)	Grand Union Canal under M4. Motorway	Dive on Green Ford Capri DNO 936G Searched. No Bodies Brentford Sec. Std By Rc 110 Brotherton Sup. 171 Kent. SCUBA

TIMES				Max Depth Metres	Remarks	Signatures of (a) Diver (b) Supervisor
Left Surface	Left Bottom	Bottom Time	Reached Surface			
1110			1132	13	10/6 Vis	(a) [signature] (b) [signature] LSM
0935			1010	3	N.I Vis	(a) [signature] (b) [signature]
1050			1120	2.5	Nil Vis	(a) [signature] (b) [signature]
						[signature]

Date	Location	Details of Operation
(16)		
3-4-84	RUSSELL ROAD	Recovery of
	RIVER LEE OVERFLOW	c/s Motor Cycles
		& Parts. OMX 774W.
		HONDA c/s IN NOV83. KUW
		111J. PUCH. Frame No
		2103790. 2 Frames.
		handed to PC 172 CHEROCTC.
		Stln by PCrMuar. Attd 198,
		24. Poss Used.
		SCUBA.
(17)		
6/4/84	Lake Commonside	Diving for shotguns
	East J/W Upper	at request of D/c Shaw
	Green East	at 1157 found Butt &
		trigger mech., at 1210.
		Found under & over sawn
		off shotgun barrel. (No
		A07970. Poss used Stby
		PC Smith. Supv. PS24 Broads
		taken to ZS. handed to
		D.I. Brooks. SCUBA

TIMES				Max Depth Metres	Remarks	Signatures of (a) Diver (b) Supervisor
Left Surface	Left Bottom	Bottom Time	Reached Surface			
1110	~~1200~~		1200	3	Nil Vis	(a) [signature]
						(b) [signature] P 24 M
1110			1210	1	Nil Vis	(a) [signature]
						(b) [signature] P24 M

Date	Location	Details of Operation
(18)		
10/4/84	West India Dock.	Search for Table Cloths. No trace. Sth By P.C. Veal . 171 Sup. Insp Johns. Pers used . SCUBA.
(19)		
13/4/84	Gunbury Reservoir Chingford.	Training Dive from rubber dingy Pers equip used 7-8ft vis signal test. repeat diver Sup PS24 Brooks St By 114 . SCUBA.
(20)		
19/4/84	Poplar BR Dock.	Training Dive Fins used. signals good vis 6 to 8ft — Sup Insp Johns. St By. P.C Veal SCUBA.

TIMES				Max Depth Metres	Remarks	Signatures of (a) Diver (b) Supervisor
Left Surface	Left Bottom	Bottom Time	Reached Surface			
1035	–	–	1110	7	1ft. Vis	(a) ...... (b) P.2.4
10-45		–	1130	10	8ft Vis	(a) ...... (b) P.2.4
1040			1130	7	20ft Vis	(a) ...... (b) P.2.4

Date	Location	Details of Operation
25/4/84 (21)	Serpentine Lake, SW Corner, Hyde Park W.2. (AH Section).	Search for Jewellery, gold ring and bracelet. Sup. 167. Attd 198 Stby 144. Pos Used. SCUBA
(22) 30/4/84	Poplar Dock Preston Road E14	Training Dive. Fins used. Pass. equip. SL by 198 Sup x PCdThu SCUBA.
(23) 3/5/84	Serpentine Lake SW Corner Hyde Park W2 (AH Section	Search for Stolen Jewellery Neg. Supr John Hughes Attd. 114-198. Fins Used SCUBA.

TIMES				Max Depth Metres	Remarks	Signatures of (a) Diver (b) Supervisor
Left Surface	Left Bottom	Bottom Time	Reached Surface			
3-40			4-40	2.5	Nil Vis.	(a) [signature]
						(b) [signature]
10⁵⁵			1140	7	2ft Vis	(a) [signature]
						(b) [signature]
10 50			1130	2.5	ft Vis.	(a) [signature]
						(b) [signature]

DIVING COURSE SUNDERLAND.

Date	Location	Details of Operation
23.5.84 (24)	DURHAM BATHS	BASIC WATER WORK NORTHUMBRIA.
24.5.84 (26)	—— " ——	—————— " ——————
29.5.84 (27)	DIVE TANK, HEXHAM	CONTROLLED ASCENTS.
30-5.84 (27)	CHAMBER, N. DOCK.	DRY DIVE
31.5.84 (30)	SOUTH DOCKS.	DIVER JACKSTAY S/BY DIVER S/BY DIVER.
1.6.84 (33)	SOUTH DOCKS SUNDERLAND	CIRCULAR SWEEP & SECTOR
2.6.84	Attended Dr. Shaws. Saw Dr. Pickworth. Diagnosed ear	infection. TO

TIMES				Max Depth Metres	Remarks	Signatures of (a) Diver (b) Supervisor
Left Surface	Left Bottom	Bottom Time	Reached Surface			
1100	1200	60	1200	3		(a) [signature] (b) [signature]
1400	1600	120	1600	3		
1045	1200	75	1200	3		(a) [signature] (b) A. Bird
1410	1610	120	1610	3		
1230	1237	11	1238	7	GOOD ASCENTS BREATHING CONTINUED	(a) [signature] (b) A. Bird
1549	1609	28	1617	10	TOTAL TIME SHOWN	(a) [signature] (b) A. Bird
1120	1209	49	1211	9	satisfactory.	(a) [signature]
1014	1015	1	1016	9.5		
1357	1358	1	1359	7.		(b) S. Hughes
1036	1123	48	1124	9	slight nose bleed	(a) [signature]
1136	1212	39	1215	8.5		(b) R. Dolby
1229	1231	2	1231	1	S. B. D.	
return		8ᵗ	inst.		NO DIVING.	[signature]

Date	Location	Details of Operation
7-6-84	POND, REAR OF WOLSINGTON HALL	WADE SEARCH
8-6-84 (34)	R TYNE, JARROW COAL STAITHES	DIVER SEARCH DAY WITH COMMUNICATIONS
11 6 84 (36)	RIVER WEAR CHESTER LE STREET	STAKE & GRID SEARCH
12-6-84 (39)	S. DOCK, SUNDERLAND	LIFTING BAG EXERCISE
13. 6.84 (41)	SOUTH DOCKS SUNDERLAND	AIR LIFT BAG. LIFTING STROP — SAFES.
14. 6 84 (43)	DERWENT RES.	Necklace Search
15. 6.84 (45)	Sea . Roker.	Direction Signals

TIMES				Max Depth Metres	Remarks	Signatures of (a) Diver (b) Supervisor
Left Surface	Left Bottom	Bottom Time	Reached Surface			
					JEWELLERY, PURSE &c	a) [signature]
					ETC. RECOVERED	b) R. Dolby
1113	1146	33	1146	12m	TOTAL TIME 44 min.	a) [signature] b) [signature]
1045	1050	5	1050	2m	S.O.D	a) [signature]
1150	1255	65	1255	2m		b) R. Dolby
1115	1118	3	1118	1m	SBD	a) [signature]
1206	1248	42	1249	8m	TOTAL TIME	b) [signature]
1256	1308	12	1310	8m	61	
1100	1135	35	1135	8M		a) [signature]
1147	1231	44	1231	8M		b) [signature]
1158	1233	35	1233	8M		a) [signature]
1430	1500	30	1500	10M		b) [signature]
1112	1200	48	1200	8		a) [signature]
1216	1305	50	1305	8		b) [signature]

Date	Location	Details of Operation
18.6.84 (46)	North Dock, chamber	Dry Dive
20.6.84 (48)	Sea Roker	Samples
21.6.84 (50)	Sea. Roker/Hendon	Depth Training
22.6.84 (52)	R. Tyne 13 sited	Lighting
26.6.84 (55)	Sea Lock. South Docks	Air Lift Pump.
27.6.84 (57)	Baths Durham	Camera Vehicle I/D Knots Trapped Diver
28.6.84 (59)	Derwent Reservoir	Depth Training

TIMES				Max Depth Metres	Remarks	Signatures of (a) Diver (b) Supervisor
Left Surface	Left Bottom	Bottom Time	Reached Surface			
1555	1615	20	1689	30M	SK	(a) [signature] (b) A Simpson
1150	1230	40	1230	10	}	(a) [signature] (b) A Bird
1442	1458	16	1458	9		
1128	1147	19	1151	19	}	(a) [signature] (b) [signature]
1445	1527	42	1527	9		
1253	1255	2	1255	6	}	(a) [signature] (b) P. [signature]
1335	1426	51	1426	6		
1145	1154	9	1154	5	}	(a) [signature] (b) [signature]
1212	1244	36	1244	5		
1408	1411	3	1411	6	ABD	
1030	1200	90	1200	3		(a) [signature] (b) [signature]
1430	1545	75	1545	3		
1326	1337	11	1345	38		(a) [signature] (b) [signature]
1455	1457	3	1458	9	Sim [illegible]	

Date	Location	Details of Operation
2.7.84 (60)	CHAMBER NORTH DOCK	DUE TO 50 M
3.7.84 (61)	RIVERSIDE QUAY R. TYNE	Comms
4.7.84 (62)	S. DOCKS, SUNDERLAND	S.D.D.E.
5.7.84 (63)	NORTH SEA S'LAND.	DEPTH TRAINING (SCUBA)
9.7.84 (65)	SEA ROKER	Depth Training
10.7.84 (68)	SOUTH DOCK	SHIPS BOTTOM SEARCH
10.7.84 (69)	NORTH DOCK	DIVER BACKSTAY
11.7.84 (70)	R. TYNE 13. SHED.	Diver Jackstay

TIMES				Max Depth Metres	Remarks	Signatures of (a) Diver (b) Supervisor
Left Surface	Left Bottom	Bottom Time	Reached Surface			
0935	0955	20	1045	50	BR2806	(a)
					TABLE 11 USED	(b)
1446	1454	10	1455	15M	retired -hole in cuff.	(a) (b) T.J. Hughes
1040	1131	54	1134	9m	TOTAL TIME SHOWN	(a) (b) ABird
1112	/	4	1116	/	UNABLE TO CLEAR EARS AT 3M.	(a) (b) T.J. Hughes
1050	1132	42	1132	8M		(a)
1450	1529	40	1529	11M		(b) AB Bird
1111	1200	49	1202	5M		(a)
1203	1205	3	1206	5M	SBD	(b) AB Bird
1256	1451	45	1454	11	Fin Recovered	(a) (b)
1337	1412	34	1412	8		(a) (b)

Date	Location	Details of Operation
19/7/84 (71)	Hampton Moorings River Thames.	Search for Boats mtr and Fire Exting: (Result all recovered) Pos wied St by. 167 · AHs 171-198 Sup. PS24 Brooks. Vis 2ft.
27/6/84 (72)	West India Dock CM Middle Dock	Search for identity of Body. (Neg Result). Pos wied. St by 171 AHs 110 Nil vis. Supr PS24
30/8/84 (73)	Welsh Harp Wood Lane NW9. (QD).	Search for M/s/for Body. Equip wied. 24 Stby. 110 & 143 attch Nil vis.

| TIMES | | | | Max Depth Metres | Remarks | Signatures of (a) Diver (b) Supervisor |
Left Surface	Left Bottom	Bottom Time	Reached Surface			
1015		55	1110	3	Recovered.	
						(a) *signature*
						(b) *signature* Ps.2.4
1022		58	1100	10	Ear clearing trouble.	(a) *signature*
						(b) *signature* Ps.2.4
2040		50	2130	1½	Recovered. Female Body.	(a) *signature* (b) *signature* Ps.2.4

Date	Location	Details of Operation
3/9/84 (74)	Regents Canal Victoria Park.	Search for Tesco Plastic Bag Cont Poss Stolen Prop. (HB). AGA used. St by AB McNICOL. Altds 198 & 114. 1ft Vis
13/9/84 (75)	West Indian Dock.	Search for sunken Motor Boat. AGA used. 198 Std by - Altds 117-114. Sup Insp Johns. Vis Nil. (HH Section)
4/10/84 (76)	Grand Union Canal Regents Row.	Search for RUCKSACK Poss Used. 110 St by D/I Pritchard Altds. 144 198 Sup 171 Vis 6in. (GH Sec)

TIMES				Max Depth Metres	Remarks	Signatures of (a) Diver (b) Supervisor
Left Surface	Left Bottom	Bottom Time	Reached Surface			
1030		60	1130	3		(a) *signature*
						(b) *signature*
1130		50	1220	7	Recovered Carried out by PLA.	(a) *signature* (b) *signature*
0950		45	1035	3.	R.	(a) *signature* (b) *signature*

Date	Location	Details of Operation
13 10/84 (77)	Grand Union Canal, Noorwood Green. Southall	Search and Recovery of Silver Honda Accord. Reg. A818 UUV recovered 1ft vis. Poss used. XN sections. Attds. 110.114. Supv.
31 10/84 (78)	Battersea Park Lake	Search for Knife used in murder. AGA used. Nil vis std by PC Hulgate Sup. PS24. (WF Section) O/Cde
1/11/84 (79)	Culvert next to Waltham Abbey	Search for Gun. AGA used nil vis slight flow std/by PC Dawson Sup PS24. DC Livingstone C8. Robbery Squad.

TIMES				Max Depth Metres	Remarks	Signatures of (a) Diver (b) Supervisor
Left Surface	Left Bottom	Bottom Time	Reached Surface			
4-20pm		20	4-40pm	3	Cow Removed by Garage.	(a) [signature] (b) Ernest [illegible]
1200		60	1300	1	No trace	(a) [signature] (b) [signature] Pozo
SSOP.						
1010		40	1050	1	No trace	(a) [signature] (b) [signature] Pozo

Date	Location	Details of Operation
2-11-84 (80)	Battersea Park Lake.	Search for Murder Weapon (Knife). AQA used. Nil vis Std by PC Newson.
27-12-84 (81)	Wapping Police Stn. Pontoon River Thames.	Clean Screw on Police Boat (new Style). Aga Used. Sty by PC SMITH. 1ft u/s
21/1/85 (1)	The New River 1 mile south of Ware, Herts.	Search for double barrelled Shotgun. AGA used. Nil vis Std by PC Annas Sup. PS24
(2)	River Thames. 250 yards Up river from Barnes Bridge	Locate & Relay Moorings. Nil vis Aga. 1½ ½ by PS24 Sup.

TIMES				Max Depth Metres	Remarks	Signatures of (a) Diver (b) Supervisor
Left Surface	Left Bottom	Bottom Time	Reached Surface			
1-30		60	2-30	1	No/Time	(a) [signature]
						(b) [signature]
1015.		15.	1030	3	Screw lever of Rape.	(a) [signature]
						(b) [signature]
1605		15.	1620	2	Shel guns recovered handed to DC Bendell YD.	(a) [signature] (b) [signature]
1100		30	1120	4	Complete	(a) [signature] (b) [signature]

Date	Location	Details of Operation
28/2/85 ③	Greenford Road. Grand Union Canal. (Thames Valey)	Search for Shotgun involved in Murder. Aqua used - Nil vis slight flow. Sup 167 Lawson. WHrs 171-144 Shtby PS24.
19 3/85 ④	Regents Canal Andrews Road opp Ash Grove E2	Search for three yellow flashing topped traffic signs Aqua used, nil vis slight flow. Sup 167. WHrs 143/198/ Shtby 144.
1 4/85 ⑤	Grand Union Canal Western Road. Southall. near Grand Junction E.H.	Search for stolen Prop. ie antiques nil, viz no flow. Aqua used. Shtby 144 Sup PC Hughes (PC97) nr.

TIMES				Max Depth Metres	Remarks	(a) (b)
Left Surface	Left Bottom	Bottom Time	Reached Surface			
1040	-	30	1110	8	Shotgun Recovered and handed to DC Light Thames Valley Police.	(a) [signature] (b) [signature] R. 16th LSM
1134		30	1206	2	Recovered x Deps at UD	(a) [signature] (b) [signature] Re 16th LSM.
1210		50	1300	2·1	No trace (to continue)	(a) [signature] (b) [signature]

Date	Location	Details of Operation
(6)		
7/4/85	St Catherines Dock London E1	Inspection & Clean of Sewer. Aqa Used.
7/4/85	Lake Maybank Park Lodge Av. Barking (KB.	Recovered Body of elderly Female.
(7)		
17/4/85	Lake Southweald Park, Brentwood Essex	Search for Proceeds of Robery. Aqa used Nil vis no flow. 110 Stby. 97 Sup - Attds 143/114.
(8)		
3/5/85	NORTHOLT INDUST ESTATE LONG DRIVE	Search for Goods Register for XS. Aqa used Nil Vis. No flow. 144 Stby 114/110. Attds. PS 46 Sup.

TIMES				Max Depth Metres	Remarks	Signatures of (a) Diver (b) Supervisor
Left Surface	Left Bottom	Bottom Time	Reached Surface			
1100		25	1125.	1	Snow Clean.	(a) [signature]
						(b) [signature] Ps24ᵗʰ
Snorkle/Wade			1		body recoval a hundred bee KD officers. (PC539ᵏ Edeman)	(a) [signature] (b) [signature]
1050		40	1130	2·1	No trace. (JW Section).	(a) [signature] (b) [signature] Pickson
1130		20	1150	2	Recovered Cash Register	(a) [signature] (b) [signature] Ps2ₐ

Date	Location	Details of Operation
8-5-85 (9)	RIVER THAMES UPPER POOL UNDER TOWER BRIDGE	SEARCH For Shotgun Aqu Used. No viz Ebb Tide (3 met). Supv 143ʳᵈ SMITH Attch 143.198 Stb By 97 DS Ball KC concerned vr case.
22-5-85 (10)	RIVER THAMES UPPER POOL UNDER TOWER BRIDGE.	SEARCH for Shotgun Aqu Used. No viz. Ebb Tide. Supv PS24ᵗʰ Brooks. Stby 143ᵗʰ Attd. 97ᵗʰ for DS Bell KC. No Trace.
3-6-85 (11)	MILLFIELD BRIDGE ROAD, RIVER LEA HOMERTON	Search for Personal Radio Aqu used No viz Supv 171 Stb by 97 Attch 114 198. for GN.

TIMES				Max Depth Metres	Remarks	Signatures of (a) Diver (b) Supervisor
Left Surface	Left Bottom	Bottom Time	Reached Surface			
1040		35	1115	7	No trace	(a) *[signature]* (b) *[signature]*
1030		45	1115	8	No trace Jabs funnel ground Cavered twice.	(a) *[signature]* (b) *[signature]*
1100		40	1140	2·1	No trace to Continue.	(a) *[signature]* (b) *[signature]*

Date	Location	Details of Operation
(12)		
20-6-85	Prince Albert Bridge Regents Canal (Cumberland Basin	Search for Gun for D/C Farmer of E.K. Aqa used. Nil viz. Supv PS24 Stg PS24 Mkd 143, 171
(13)		
6-8-85	Tit tube, Allum Farm, Southend Road.	Search for M/Cycle & Parts. Handcuff P/Stn 10' viz. Posi used. Sup PS24. Stf kg. 167 Lawson
9-8-85	Aldenham Reservoir Watford	Search for missing female. (SD) Wade & swim out to body found floating. Sup 97.
12-8-85	Lloyds Park Forest Rd E7.	Search for missing child. Snorkle. with PS24 m Brooks.

TIMES				Max Depth Metres	Remarks	Signatures of (a) Diver (b) Supervisor
Left Surface	Left Bottom	Bottom Time	Reached Surface			
1155		45	1240	3	No trace to Continue	(a) [signature] (b) [signature] P. 2w
11-55		50	1245	4	M/Cycle Recovered.	(a) [signature] (b) [signature] P. 2w
					Female Body found & handed to PC 3795 Harvey	(a) [signature] [signature]
					No trace	(a) [signature] [signature] Prw

	Date	Location	Details of Operation
(14)	15/8/85	River Lea. Homerton Road Hackney.	Dive for Guns in River Lea Aqua used, Stilley 171. Super lamp John. VMtds 114 & 143. 1ft viz to Nil viz. No Flow.
(15)	20-8-85	River Thames Dummy e/s UD. Search for launch	Search for Rudder of Launch. Posidon Used. Stilley 97 VMtds 143, 110 144. Super. 110. Nil viz. 2 Knot Flow.
(16)		Bow Road M/R Elsdene River Lea.	Search for P Radio Aqua Used Stilley 143 Smith. VMtd 144 super 24. Slight flow nil viz thick mud bottom. Res used.

TIMES				Max Depth Metres	Remarks	Signatures of (a) Diver (b) Supervisor
Left Surface	Left Bottom	Bottom Time	Reached Surface			
1030		60	1130	30	No trace to Continue	(a) [signature] (b) [signature]
1100		55	1155	4	No trace	(a) [signature] (b) [signature]
1105		65	1210	4	No trace to Continue	(a) [signature] (b) [signature]

Date	Location	Details of Operation
3/9/85 (17)	Crykley Heads Deelan	Trapped dive Band mask
24/9/85 (18)	Tyne Dock	Training. S.C.U.B.A.
9-9-85 (19)	TYNE DOCK	S.D.D.E. TRAINING
10/9/85 (19 & 20)	Mill Buoy Herdon Sea Roker Pier	Depth training Signals.
11.9.85 (21)	NORTH SEA OFF. SUNDERLAND	DEPTH TRAINING & ROPE SIGNALS SCUBA SIM DEC STOPS
12-9-85 (22)	CHAMBER, N. DOCK	DRY DIVE, NARCOSIS TEST

TIMES				Max Depth Metres	Remarks	Signatures of (a) Diver (b) Supervisor
Left Surface	Left Bottom	Bottom Time	Reached Surface			
1030	1200	90	1200	3		(a)
1400	1545	105	1545	3		(b)
1410	1500	50	1500	11		(a) (b)
1532	1628	56	1630	8m	KIRBY morgan	(a) (b)
1130	1143	13	1148	21		(a)
1306	1337	51	1400	8		(b)
1132	1143	11	1147	39.	O.K. SIM DEC STPS 5 MIN 3 MTRS.	(a) (b) J. Hughes
1440	1500	20	1522	30 MT	6 MT STOP – 5 MIN 3 MT STOP – 5 MIN	(a) (b) A. Bird

Date	Location	Details of Operation
16/9/85 (23)	River Thames Under Southwark Bridge.	Search for sawn off Shotgun. Aqa used Std by PC110. Attd. 24, 97, Supv Insp John. 2 knot tide Nil viz
20/9/85 (24)	Surrey Basin Branch 8L Rotherhithe	Search for missing 7 year old girl. Aqa Pos used. Std by 110. Attd 114, 24, Supv Insp J. Nil vis Temp 66F
26/9/85 (25)	Victoria Dock Between warehouse B & C.	Search for Missing Keighley Barton (14 yrs old) Aqa Used. Std by PC167 Lawson supv 114. Nil Viz Nil currents. Water temp 19c

TIMES				Max Depth Metres	Remarks	Signatures of (a) Diver (b) Supervisor
Left Surface	Left Bottom	Bottom Time	Reached Surface			
1035		45	1120	8	No trace to Continue	(a) [signature]
						(b) [signature]
1625		45	1710	4	No trace to Continue	(a) [signature]
						(b) [signature]
1205		25	1230	10	No trace to Continue	(a) [signature]
						(b) J. A. Newsan

[signature]

Date	Location	Details of Operation
11/10/85 (26)	Royal Victoria Dock.	Search for missing child Keighley Bowtain. Aqu used. Attds 198 + Jnp J. Stby 114. Nil Vis Nil current. Water temp 19 C
12/10/85 (27)	WILLIAM GIRLING RESERVOIR. CHINGFORD	Search for missing Anchor (TWA). Pos used. S.lby 167 - Attds. 171 x 143. Snp. 171 20' vis No Current. Water temp 17'
22/10/85 (28)	River Lea, Bow Flyover.	Search for Handgun (JB) Aqu used. Snpv143 Smith Attds 143/114. Stblny 198. Nil vis, slight current Water Temp 62 F.

TIMES				Max Depth Metres	Remarks	Signatures of (a) Diver (b) Supervisor
Left Surface	Left Bottom	Bottom Time	Reached Surface			
0940		45	1025	10	Dark Colour Citroen found No No Plates	(a) [signature] (b) [signature]
1110		30	1140	9	No trace to Continue	(a) [signature] (b) [signature]
1055		45	1140	2	No trace to Continue	(a) [signature] (b) Ernest Smith

Date	Location	Details of Operation
29 10/6. (29)	Victoria Park. Spillers Cut. East Side	Search for Body in M/V. Vehicle Buhr Aqua used. Supr 167 Lawson. Stby 143 Altds 198-167. Nil Viz No current.
(30) 18 11/85	Littleton Sailing Club. Littleton Lake.	Check out submerged Motor Vehicle. Aqua used. Supr lmp Johns. Stby 114, altds 198 143 171. 3 ft Viz. no curr 8°C Temp.
1986 (1) 2 1/86.	River Lea. Walpus Road Hackney.	Search for missing 19 year old girl Aqua used Stby 143 Altds 171-144 Supr lmp Johns. Nil viz (Alison Day).

TIMES				Max Depth Metres	Remarks	Signatures of (a) Diver (b) Supervisor
Left Surface	Left Bottom	Bottom Time	Reached Surface			
9·51		37	1028	7 mts	No trace. Rubbish & bottom. to Continue	(a) [signature] (b)
1040		40	1120	4 mts	Bluey Mini found. No No plate	(a) [signature] (b) [signature]
1005		55	1100	3 mts	No trace to Continue	(a) [signature] (b) [signature]

Date	Location	Details of Operation
(2)		
13/1/86	River Lea. Hackney.	Search for missing 19 year old girl. Aqa used Altds 198 114, SM by 143 Sup + 171 Ked. No flow Nil viz temp. 48F. (Allison Day)
(3)		
22-1-86	River Lea Hackney	Search for clothing relating to Body found. (19 year old girl) Pos Used. St By 110. Altds. 97-143. Sup 171 No flow 0-2ft viz. Temp 47. (Alison Day)
(4)		
30-1-86	River Lea Eastway Bridge	Search for clothing re Body found (19 year old girl). Aqa used St by 114, Altds 167-171 No viz Tep 44 (Alison Day)

TIMES				Max Depth Metres	Remarks	Signatures of (a) Diver (b) Supervisor
Left Surface	Left Bottom	Bottom Time	Reached Surface			
1030		45.	1115.	3	No trace. await further info. Body found 171. Strangled & hands tied in front. half naked.	(a) [signature] (b) [signature]
1050		45.	1155	3	No trace. Clothing.	(a) [signature] (b) [signature] 171
1030 ~~#5.~~		45.	1115	3	No trace. Shoes. Clothing found.	(a) [signature] (b) [signature]

Date	Location	Details of Operation
12/2/86 (5)	River Lea Cooks Ferry Inn	(YE Section). Search for head of headless body found previous day. AGA used. Stby 144. Attds. 143 - 110. Sup. Insp. Johns Water temp 1c Ice on Surface 2" thick.
20/2/86 (6)	River Lea Cooks Ferry Inn	YE Section. Search for head and Carpet from car. Azen used Stby 145 - Attds 110. Sup. 167. Water temp 1c Ice on Surface 3" thick
6/3/86 (7)	King George IV Reservoir STAINS . MIDDX	(Regional Dive) Search for alledged exp devices Pos Used. Stby 144 Attds 110 171 Supv PS24 15 ft viz

TIMES				Max Depth Metres	Remarks	Signatures of (a) Diver (b) Supervisor
Left Surface	Left Bottom	Bottom Time	Reached Surface			
1110		45	1155	4	No have to Continue Dive under ice . 1°c .	(a) [signature] (b) [signature]
1224		27	1251	4	Compet found taken by CID & SOCCO Marked MM/1 Dive under ice .	(a) [signature] (b) [signature]
1330		60	1430	~~16~~ 16	(1) explosive device on chain located . (1) exp device under pontoon	(a) [signature] (b) [signature]

Date	Location	Details of Operation
8-3-86 (8)	Serpentine Hyde Park.	Periodic Search. Poss Used. Stl by .144. Attds 171 Supv 167.
26/3/86 (9)	Grand Union Canal Edwin Rd Harlesden	Search for stolen prop. Vgu used. Stby 97. Attds 144 Supv Insp Johns
(10) 4/4/86	River Longford Hanworth Park Forest Road Feltham (Culvert & tunnel)	Search for stolen BMX Bikes Poss Used Stby 143 (114, 144 attds) Supv 167. Nill Vis No Plun. Info WPC 688 co

TIMES				Max Depth Metres	Remarks	Signatures of (a) Diver (b) Supervisor
Left Surface	Left Bottom	Bottom Time	Reached Surface			
1227		48	1-15p	3	Good vis nothing of interest	(a) [signature] (b) AGL R.162
1045		60	1145	3	1 item rec to continue	(a) [signature] (b)
1031		16	1047	6'	No trace	(a) [signature] (b) AGL R.162

Date	Location	Details of Operation
(11) 16/4/86	River Thames	Search for Gold under Tug app'd O/D. Pos Used. Super hrd John St/by. J.Hughes Attch 143 114.
(12) 23/4/86	Lake rear of Chiswick House Park Road W4.	Search for Handgun. Re: Ant. Terrorist squad. (Ds Bell c13). Pos Used. St/by 167. Super 198. Attd. 171.
(13) 3/7/86	River Lea 100 yds North Bakers Hill E5.	Check out submerged car. Pos Used. attch. 114 143 St/By 24. Super 167. 1fh. viz.
(14) 13/5/86	Paddington Arm (Canal) begin Harrow Road Bridge	Search for H/Bags Agen. Used St/by 24, Attch 198 144, Sup 167 ™ N.I viz

TIMES				Max Depth Metres	Remarks	Signatures of (a) Diver (b) Supervisor
Left Surface	Left Bottom	Bottom Time	Reached Surface			
1230		30	1300	5	No trace	(a) [signature]
						(b) [signature]
1200		60	1300	2	Handgun Recover.	(a) [signature]
						(b) [signature]
1013		11	1024	2	Orange Ford Escort. UHY383H L/S RD.	(a) [signature] (b) [signature]
1012		48	1100	2	N/T to Continue.	(a) [signature] (b) [signature]

Date	Location	Details of Operation
17/5/86 (15)	Grand Union Canal. Harrow Road,	Search for Handbags. Aqua used. S/by 167 Vehcls 97, 110, 144 Sup 24. Nil viz N.V.C.
30/5/86 (16)	Regents Canal Andrews St.	Search for Browning Auto Pistol for HB S/by 114, Aqua used. Vehcls 144, 198, Sup. 24. Nil to 6" viz N.V.C.
13/6/86 (17)	River Thames Gallow Barge down stream from river Thames	Search for Missing Person (drowning) Poss Used. S/by 114 Vehcls 97, 110 Sup. lwy Johns. Nil viz strong current.

TIMES				Max Depth Metres	Remarks	Signatures of (a) Diver (b) Supervisor
Left Surface	Left Bottom	Bottom Time	Reached Surface			
1120		50	1210	3	No trace. H/B. Purses found.	(a) [signature] Rea (b) [signature] R24
1100		60	1200	3	N/T to Continue.	(a) [signature] (b) [signature] R24
1250		70	1310	3	Recovered Male body	(a) [signature] (b) [signature]

Date	Location	Details of Operation
21-6-86 (18)	Limehouse Cut - Bridge at Burdett Rd.	Search for Video & Camerize clocks (re murder enq.). Pos used Stby 110. Abtds 97 171. Super 171.
2/7/86 (19)	Daylin Survey & Train Dive Luxborough Lake Chigwell	Diving Operation Daylin survey Pos used. (Abtds 198 144 Stby 167 Super 198 2ft vis
6/7/86 (18)	Shoreham 1 mile SE Shoreham Light-house. (BSAC DIVE).	Dive with Bexley BSAC in Sea. Pos used. Buddy diver Tony Smith.
(19)	Rest M TOWN 1 mile Sth Shoreham L/House	Dive Bex BSAC Poss used. Buddy Diver - Tony Smith

BSAC DIVE

TIMES				Max Depth Metres	Remarks	Signatures of (a) Diver (b) Supervisor
Left Surface	Left Bottom	Bottom Time	Reached Surface			
1130		40	1210'	3	N/T to Cauline	(a) [signature]
						(b) [signature] 17¹
1153		50	1243	6	— Gravel & Clay bottom. various bus.	(a) [signature] (b) J. Astyako
0930		52	1022	12	Good Viz	(a) [signature]
1410		48	1458	10	Good Viz	(a) [signature]

Date	Location	Details of Operation
9/7/86 (20)	Vau River Vicinity at Lordship Lane.	Search for various Firearms (Poss) DC Randall COC8. Pars Used. St by 167 Attds 97 198 Sup. 198. Slight flow.
28/7/86 (21) (22)	Gravel Pit. Stockley Park West Drayton	Search for jacket & trousers. X E section Poss Used. St by 116 Attds 97 146 Supr 24. 1A 613
5/8/86 (23)	River Thames Wandsworth Bridge SW16	Search for Rifle Aga used St by 198 Attds 167, 146. Supr 167. Nil vis. 2 kind current EE section

TIMES				Max Depth Metres	Remarks	Sig (a) D (b) St_
Left Surface	Left Bottom	Bottom Time	Reached Surface			
10 27		80'	1147	1.5	No Trace.	(a)
						(b)
1135		25	1200	3	N/T	(a)
1230		30	1300	3	N/T	
						(b) P.24
9.31		53	10.24	8	N/T to Continue	(a)
						(b) P.24

Date	Location	Details of Operation
13/8/86 (24)	STOCKLEY ROAD LAKE (near Heathrow)	Search for Rucksack. Aga Used. Sthy PS24 Brooks. Alts 114, 142, 6ft viz. to nil. Lot of weed. No flow. Buddy to PC Kemp. Supr 24
4/9/86 (25)	Paliakastritsa. Corfu. (sea)	Pleasure dive in Ionean Sea. Pos Used. Dived with Mr Blackman 20ft gloss viz.
12/9/86 (26)	Andrews Road, No2. E8 Regents Canal.	Dive for Bag & Contents seen to be thrown into Canal. Aga Used. Sthy PC Smith. Supr PS24 N.I Viz, n.i current Supr PS24

TIMES				Max Depth Metres	Remarks	Signatures of (a) Diver (b) Supervisor
Left Surface	Left Bottom	Bottom Time	Reached Surface			
1130		50	1220	4	N/T.	(a)
						(b)
1430		35	1505	20	tompin sea life. Depth gague used.	(a)
1040		50	1130	3	Nothing of Interest found	(a)
						(b)

Date	Location	Details of Operation
20/9/86 (27)	Search for Knives & Clothing Re murder. Regent Canal. Canal Road Mile End E3	Search in Saturday [illegible] Aqua Used, Standby PC 114 Newsan Attds. 198, 144, 167. Search in Nil viz will Commd Supr PC 167 Lawson
2/10/86 (28)	Lake Ashford Way STAINES	Check out submerged Car for PC 344 Lawrence TCG. Aqua Used. Sthg PC 97 Hughes. Attds 143 167 Supr 24 Brooks.
17/10/86 (29)	Ships Bottom Search on Celtic Surveyor	Pas used. Colifor Saturday Search with 114 Newson. 2ft viz Search OK. Supr PS 24. Attds 144 143.

TIMES				Max Depth Metres	Remarks	Signatures of (a) Diver (b) Supervisor
Left Surface	Left Bottom	Bottom Time	Reached Surface			
1154		49	1243	2	No trace to Continue	(a) [signature] (b) [signature]
1120		10.	1130	3	While 1100 Reg 561 FW L. N/T Low Stolen Been in for long time	(a) [signature] (b) [signature] P 524
1040		25.	1110	5	Search OK No Banks.	(a) [signature] (b) [signature] P 525

Date	Location	Details of Operation
(30)		Dive on Ships Bottom ("Cavalier")
22-10-86	Brighton Marina Search for explosives on ("Cavalier")	in Brighton Marina Poss Used Jackstay search 0 to 6in Viz Vfldh 97, 166 8hky 167 · Supo 145 Smith
(31) & (32)		
26-10-86	BSAC Dive at GILDENBURGH WATER WHITTLESEY, NEAR PETERBOROUGH.	Diving exercise for Dive Leader qualification Open Water Rescue skills and Air sharing. teamed with Nick Taylor. Instructor Tony SMITH. Poss used. 2ft viz.

TIMES				Max Depth Metres	Remarks	Signatures of (a) Diver (b) Supervisor
Left Surface	Left Bottom	Bottom Time	Reached Surface			
1225		35.	1pm	5	Weed and Barnacles to bilge keel. hex clean. (Reserve pulled)	(a) [signature] (b) [signature]
1200		12.	1212	20	(Bouyant lift)	(a) [signature]
1328.		12.	1340	20	Controlled bouyant lift and ENA, so into tow then CM. & EMA. No problem.	(b) A P Smith C 1 2 847.

Date	Location	Details of Operation
11/86 (53)	River Thames Lower Ham Road Richmond	Search for Machine tools for British Aerospace. Rtga Used. Slky 144. Altds 97 110. Supv Insp Johns. Slight flow. Nil viz.
21/11/86 (34)(35)	Aykley Heads Durham	Trapped diver
25.11.86 (36)	North Dock. R. Wear	EXERCISE - FOUL PROP. SCUBA
27-11-86 (37)	Fatfield Slip. R. Wear.	SUPERVISOR EXERCISE. SCUBA.

TIMES				Max Depth Metres	Remarks	Signatures of (a) Diver (b) Supervisor
Left Surface	Left Bottom	Bottom Time	Reached Surface			
1025		55	1120	5	No time to Continue	(a) [signature]
						(b) [signature]
1030	1200	90	1200	3	Dug in Klug	[signature]
1410	1530	80	1530	3	to use open mouthpiece	[signature]
1558			1603	4m.	Prop cleared	(a) [signature] (b) [signature]
1217	1219	2	1219	2	S30	(a) [signature] (b) [signature]

Date	Location	Details of Operation
8-12-86 (38)	Bedfont Lake. Bedfont Road. Feltham Middx	Search for Canning Fork used in Murder FT Agg used 144 Stdby. Wkd 198 Super 143. Nil viz no flow.
18/12/86 (39)	River Thames Battersea Rail Bridge	Search for Murder Agg used. Stky 143. Wkts 114 143/67 Super 8524. Nil viz 2 Knot flow.
1987 (1)	Shadwell Basin Glamis Road.	Search for ring. Pos used. Stky 114, Wkts 92 110 143 Super twp John. Nil viz no flow

TIMES				Max Depth Metres	Remarks	Signatures of (a) Diver (b) Supervisor
Left Surface	Left Bottom	Bottom Time	Reached Surface			
1115		60	1215	3	Nt to Continue	(a) _[signature]_
						(b) _[signature]_
0930		45	1015	4		(a) _[signature]_
						(b) _[signature]_ P324
9-20		40	1000	7	Nt to Continue	(a) _[signature]_
						(b) _[signature]_

Date	Location	Details of Operation
10-1-87 ②	River Thames, Chertsey Bridge	Dive for missing car. Aga used. Sky J. Smith Attd. 167, 146, Supv24. 6in Viz 2knot flow. Police Boat used.
4/3/87 ③ ✓	Luxborough Lake. Luxborough Lane. Chigwell. (BSAC Dive).	Assessment Dive for Dive Leader. Acting as Dive Leader, leading Novice Diver (Inst Neil Webb) an 1st O/W Dive. Qual Dive 9.
4/3/87 ④ ✓	Luxborough Lake. Luxborough Lane. Chigwell (BSAC Dive)	Assessment Dive for Dive Leader qualification. Dive Leader leading Sports Diver (Inst Neil Webb) an O/W dive. Q Dive 8

TIMES				Max Depth Metres	Remarks	Signatures of (a) Diver (b) Supervisor
Left Surface	Left Bottom	Bottom Time	Reached Surface			
					Car Panel. Austin Maestro	(a) [signature]
1045.		15.	1100	5.	Red BPK4154 No Body.	
						(b) [signature] P.124
1345		20	1405.	6	2ft Viz snow fresh water. Temp 4°C	(a) [signature]
						(b) [signature] CI 34432
						(a) [signature]
1420		17	1437	15.	1ft to Nil Viz fresh water 4°C	(b) [signature] CI 34432

Date	Location	Details of Operation
22/3/87 (5)	Stoney Cove. (BSAC Dive)	Assessment Dive for Dive Leader. Leading Nial Webb Wubular (Acting as Sports Diver) Compass Navigation to Coach (240°) from Landing Stage. Found Coach, Toilet - Rail Pole & Cock Pit of Plane.
22/3/87 (6)	Stoney Cove. (BSAC Dive)	Dive with Nick Taylor Compass navigation used. Acted as dive Leader. Found: Welding Platform Lift Bucket, Boiler surfaced on slipway.
30/3/87 (7)	Kings Reach R. Thames opp Bulls Wharf.	Search for Lost engine Viz a used. Slky. PS 24m Wbd. 110. 143. Surg 110 Brothal — ND U. 3 3 Knt flow.

TIMES				Max Depth Metres	Remarks	Signatures of (a) Diver (b) Supervisor
Left Surface	Left Bottom	Bottom Time	Reached Surface			
					Remarkable viz about	(a) [signature]
1045	1105	20	1109	22	12 foot	
						(b) [signature]
1158		18	1216	22	good viz.	(a) [signature]
						(b) [signature]
1050		35	1125	4	Nil viz 3 knot flow. bowed search line to continue	(a) [signature] (b) [signature]

Date	Location	Details of Operation
18-4-87 (8)	River Thames Lower Hampton Road	Search for Knife Aga used. 5t kg. 114 Nawson Attels 97 Hughes x 167 Lawson Supr 24 Brooks Nil to bin viz. slight flow.
10-5-87 (9)	Seaford. Marine Parade. Opp Buckle Inn Car park. (Sea Dive BSAC)	Dive from shore intn Crbs smaller squid. and hermit crabs. 3 to 4 ft. viz. Poss used slight flow. SMB x Comp Nav used.
10-5-87 (10)	Seaford. Marine Parade. Opp Buckle Inn Car Park. (Sea Dive BSAC.	Dive from shore all Crbs Spitter (SD) Over rocks. Crabs small, nothing of interest. 2-3 ft viz Poss used. SMB used

TIMES				Max Depth Metres	Remarks	Signatures of (a) Diver (b) Supervisor
Left Surface	Left Bottom	Bottom Time	Reached Surface			
1015.		45.	1100	3	Area Searched. No trace Jackstay used.	(a) [signature] (b) [signature]
11.12.		31	1143	7	Mostly Sand. uninteresting	(a) [signature] (b) [signature]
1300		25.	1425	5.	Rocks & small Crabs boring!	(a) [signature] (b) [signature]

Date	Location	Details of Operation
12/5/87 (11)	Millwall Basin West India Dock	Search for M/V seen to go into Dock. Aqa Used Std By 198 Halcyné Mtrs 143 x 144. Surp. Insp Johns. 1ft to nil viz.
16/5/87 (12)	Regents Canal Mile End Road. Bridge (HH)	Search for Hammer, Knife and Red leather Books. for HH CID. Aqa used Std By 167. Lawson Altd 144 410. Supv 24 1ft to nil viz.
24/5/87 (13)	SS. LOUIS SHED. OFF THURLSTON SANDS Salcombe Devon BUILT AS A TRAMP STEAMER IN 1939. (BSAC)	Boat Dive with Karen Spreadbury. Acting as D/L dived her with compass nav. to SS LOUIS SHED. GOOD VIZ. Poss wreck nice fish lots of crabs. not much left on wreck

TIMES				Max Depth Metres	Remarks	Signatures of (a) Diver (b) Supervisor
Left Surface	Left Bottom	Bottom Time	Reached Surface			
1000		45	1045	8	Found 4 Cars Ford Escort white Morris Oxford. Rolls Royce Rsy 32 KX & Renault	(a) [signature] (b) [signature]
1010		70	1120	3	Nothing found	(a) [signature] (b) [signature]
1245.		45	1330	10	Enjoyable. Dive Raven Spreadbury good Standby Partner.	(a) [signature] (b) [signature] Dm

Date	Location	Details of Operation
25/5/87 (14)	Challaborough Bigbury Bay Devon. Dive on SS Persier. 5,382 ton Steam. Built 1982. (BSAC)	Dive with Simone STEADMAN from boat onto SS Persier 2 miles out to sea. Acting as D/L we found the wreck. Started from bows and examined part of wreck. good viz lots of marine fish. rec for dive. Pos used. No SMB.
27/5/87 (15)	Dive on Wreck 'Jebba' Hope Cove, Bolt Head Salcombe. (BSAC)	Dive with Joe Jackson from inflatable. Myself as D/L. Wreck not found but nice reef. lots of fish, crabs etc. Pos used. 10ft viz

TIMES				Max Depth Metres	Remarks	Signatures of (a) Diver (b) Supervisor
Left Surface	Left Bottom	Bottom Time	Reached Surface			
						(a)
					Good dive	
1253		20	1317	30	Simon good	
					partner,	
					although find	
					him a	(b)
					little fast	
1100		47	1147	10	Enjoyable	(a)
					Dive joe	
					good steady	
					diver.	
						(b)

Date	Location	Details of Operation
27/5/87 (16) ✓	Dive on Tekken Hope Cove.	Dive with Joe Jackson acting as dive leader. eventually traced the wreck. Tekken spread over a large area and covered in kelp. Poor vis. good viz.
28/5/87 (17) ✓	Dive on Hertzogin Cecile in Starr with Hole Bay, South sand	Acting as D/L. dived with Tony Destefina and Cris Suitter on wreck Cecile not much left of wreck saw large wrass, big Conger eel. good viz. saw large Conger. Kelp rocks & sand. Bottom. good viz.

TIMES				Max Depth Metres	Remarks	Signatures of (a) Diver (b) Supervisor
Left Surface	Left Bottom	Bottom Time	Reached Surface			
1630		57	1727	12	Enjoyable Dive – good viz. Dave a steady person to dive with. reliable	(a) [signature] (b) [signature] DM.
1530		52	1622	9	Enjoyable dive. Two good partners to dive with although I prefer diving in pairs, as most time taken up keeping watch over other divers.	(a) [signature] (b) [signature] DM

Date	Location	Details of Operation
29/5/87 (18)	Dive on SS PERSIER. Challaborough, Bigbury Bay (BSAC -)	Acting as D/L with SMB. Paul Tony. down the anchor rope which was directly on the wreck. Last used. viz about 10 feet rec as good dive unfortunately not enough bottom time to see all wreck.
2/6/87 19	South Quay Millwall Dock	Dive looking for hinge. Aqua went Sthy 167 Lawson Attils 97 & 198 Super 24 Brooks. 6" to nil viz. 7°c. No current.

TIMES				Max Depth Metres	Remarks	Signatures of (a) Diver (b) Supervisor
Left Surface	Left Bottom	Bottom Time	Reached Surface			
1551		20	1611	30	Marvelous dive like being in an aquarium lots of fish. Wreck very much intact. Tony good buddy, steady & sensible.	(a) [signature] (b) [signature] Dm.
1030	1110	40	1111	9.	Nr.	(a) [signature] (b) [signature]

Date	Location	Details of Operation
23/6/87 (20)	MILLWALL DOCK SOUTH QUAY PLAZA	SEARCH & RECOVERY OF BLACK PONTIAC. Aqua used. Std by 143 search. Attds 97, 110, 198 Supv. PS24 Book - Nil viz. No flow.
2/7/87 (21)	River Thames Ham, Sandy Lane Richmond	Search for Possible Car in Thames Aqua used Stby 97 Attds 198, 114, 144, 167. Supv. 24 Slight flow 1ft viz
15/7/87 (22)	Shadwell Basin Glamis Road Wapping	Search for Explosives in Shadwell Basin Prior to visit by P. Charles Aqa used Stby 24 Attds 143, 144, 198. Supv Insp John 2ft viz. No flow.

TIMES				Max Depth Metres	Remarks	Signatures of (a) Diver (b) Supervisor
Left Surface	Left Bottom	Bottom Time	Reached Surface			
1150		30	1220	9.	Con Black Pontine Reg. Recovered. by Crane	(a) [signature] (b) [signature] Pozzi[?]
11-15		60	1215	3	Anchor ~~found lump~~ ~~forced, Canoe~~ ~~found~~	(a) [signature] (b) [signature] Pozzi[?]
0730 ~~0825~~		50	0820	5	Security Search for Explosive N/T fortunately	(a) [signature] (b) [signature]

Date	Location	Details of Operation
26/7/87 (23)	Sea, off Goring Worthing Sussex	Drift Dive looking for wreck Lydwina not found. ended up Drift Dive with Steve Fuller. not very interesting Cowshelf used. Strong flow.
30/7/87 (24)	Security Search WEST INDIA DOCK re Queens opening of Docklands railway	Search for Poss Explosives on support of Docklands light - Rail way Viga used. Sty 97 White's 1 & 167 No flow. Ift Viz. Sup prop Inflatables used.
30/7/87 (25)	Security Search Greenwich Pier re Queens Open of Docklands Railway	Search for explosives under Greenwich Pier Viga used. Sty 97 White's 167 Sup v. Insp J. Strong flow nil viz.

TIMES				Max Depth Metres	Remarks	Signatures of (a) Diver (b) Supervisor
Left Surface	Left Bottom	Bottom Time	Reached Surface			
				12		(a)
						(b)
0845		60	0945.	9.	NT Fortunately	(a)
						(b)
1045.		20	1105.	2	No tvne. river clear	(a)
						(b)

Date	Location	Details of Operation
4/8/87 (26)	Grand Union Canal. Park Road NW8.	Dive for Knife re suicide from 150ft Crane by Iranian Muslem as he fell Knife went into Canal. Aqua Used. Stby PS24 Wtd. 146, Supy 167 slight flaw nil viz.
11/9/87 (27)	River Thames Middx shore near Kingston Bridge	Dive for Shotgun for TR Aqua used. Std By 110, Wtds 114 - 148, Supy 114, Nil Viz No flow.
15/9/87 (28)	River Lee Spring Hill E5.	Search for ½ million in Giro cheques etc, in blue Plastic Bag. Aqua Used Stby 110. Wtds 2497,146,114 Super Insp J. Nil viz.

| TIMES | | | | Max Depth Metres | Remarks | Signatures of
(a) Diver
(b) Supervisor |
Left Surface	Left Bottom	Bottom Time	Reached Surface			
1:22 pm		36	1:58 pm	2.	Knife used — found to continue	(a) [signature]
		36				
						(b) [signature]
1123		41	1204	3.4	No dive to continue	(a) [signature]
						(b) g.a. Dawson 114
1020		35.	1055	3.	No dive.	(a) [signature]
						(b)

Date	Location	Details of Operation
18/9/87 (29)	St Catherines Dock London.	Search in St Cats Dock Periodical. Aga used. Stby 146. Attds 114, 144, Supv. 114, Nil Viz.
28/9/87 (30) (31)×(32)	Plough Way Greenland Dock, SE16.	Search of Upturned Dredger for Poss Body & Surrounding Area Aga used Stby 144 Ducas Attds 146, 198, 24, Stby Supv. Ins Johns
5/10/87 (33)	Sea, Muxton Hole off Selsea Bill (BSAC)	Dive in sea from Inflatable good weather hardly any flow buddies Mick Collins and Steve Clark. mainly bottom, plenty of life most enjoyable dive Conshelf, 21 used.

TIMES				Max Depth Metres	Remarks	Signatures of (a) Diver (b) Supervisor
Left Surface	Left Bottom	Bottom Time	Reached Surface			
1042		26	1108	4.6	Bottom Board found to owner on scene	(a) [signature] (b) [signature]
1910		10	1920	8	2ft Viz. torch used. nil current Cab clear of bottom. searched w/t of Bodies.	(a) [signature] (b) [signature]
1930		20	1950	8		
2100		15	2115	8		
1345		30	1416	20	good vig at bottom to feel. two good buddies Lots of lobsters & crabs.	(a) [signature] M Collins (b)

Date	Location	Details of Operation
17¹⁰/87 (34)	River Thames Wapping Police Boat Yard.	Search for ladder. lost (Poss). Aqua used. SHby. Lt Show. Whb. 143-167 Supr KS24 Broaks. 3 kut flow. N.I viz.
5/11/87 (35)	K.G.5 London Dock	Security Search for explosive devices under M/V Moore re Visit of Queen to Stall Part. Aqua Used. SHby 97, Whb 143, 167. Supr Twip J. No flow. 2ft viz.
12/11/87 (36)	Woolwich Aquatic Centre. (DRY DOCK)	Dive with D Hawstor. Practicing bouyant assent and Emre. Poss used. Buddy sharing. 4 to 8ft viz. no flow.

TIMES				Max Depth Metres	Remarks	Signatures of (a) Diver (b) Supervisor
Left Surface	Left Bottom	Bottom Time	Reached Surface			
1000		50	1050	9	N/T to Continue	(a) [signature] (b) [signature]
1200		15	1215	2	N/T fortunately for me.	(a) [signature] (b) [signature]
1120		40	1200	8	Good Drill Carried out by . D. Hoskin Cofident diver reliable buddy in any situation	(a) [signature] (b)

Date	Location	Details of Operation
271187	HMS VERNON	CC DIVE
271187	— '' —	EMERGENCY SURFACE DRILLS
271187	— '' —	TBU BOLT GUN / VIXEN U/W CUT
271187	— '' —	BUCKET DIVE
(37)	''	Diving with Royal
(38)	''	Engineers Portsmouth
(39)	''	use of Tornado T60
(40)	''	Bolt gun and Vixen.
	''	Hydrogen Oxygen, Aquarius
		used. two equalization.
27-11-87	Horsea Lake	Night Dive and
(41)	Portsmouth.	Jonny Jackstay search
		with John Smith.
		(Av Diver). 10ft viz.
		Sea water lake. good
		life. Aquarius used.
28-11-87	Royal Navy	
(42)	Training Tank.	Dive with E Smith.
	Dive with Decom	No clear surface. Dive
	Stops.	2 Decom Stops
		Aquarius used.

| TIMES | | | | Max Depth Metres | Remarks | Signatures of (a) Diver (b) Supervisor |
Left Surface	Left Bottom	Bottom Time	Reached Surface			
		30	35		Decom Stopes at 6m x 3m	SNCO Instr RE Diving Estab
		20	5			SNCO Instr RE Diving Esta
		60	5			SNCO Instr RE Diving Estab
		05	5			SNCO Instr RE Diving Estab
					3ft Viz pressure waves from T60 guns cutter very noisey.	(a)
1010 pm		50	1100 pm	7	good dive	(a)
						(b)
1000 am		55	1055	20	Decompression Stop on shot 3m for 5mins	(a)
						(b)

Date	Location	Details of Operation
29/11/87 (43)	Stoney Cove Leicestershire (BSAC).	Dive with Loraine Cook Novice Diver. found Aircraft and saw lots of fish. good viz stoney bottom. Pas used. water cold
29/11/87 (44)	Stoney Cove Leicestershire (BSAC.)	Dive with Mathew Freeman Sports Diver His first time in open water with Dry Suit. good Control good viz. stoney Bottom Cold. Pas Used.
2/12/87 (45)	Serpentine Hyde Park London	Periodical Search. Std by 144 with 198, 143. No flow nil viz. Supervison Insp. J. Argue used. water cold.

TIMES				Max Depth Metres	Remarks	Signatures of (a) Diver (b) Supervisor
Left Surface	Left Bottom	Bottom Time	Reached Surface			
10 47		28	1115	12	Lannie still learning cofidout, responded to out of air sign well. stays close and understands well. (b) = other Diver.	(a) [signature] (b) [signature]
1150		25	1215	18	Good Diver. controlled Dry Suit well consid first time in openwater. (b) other Diver.	(a) [signature] (b) M freeman
~~1105~~ 1025		40	1105.	4	Camera famil. of nature.	(a) [signature] (b) [signature]

Date	Location	Details of Operation
14/1/88 ①	Canal, Limehouse Cut, Violet Road.	Search for firearms. Aqa used, stand by PC 144, PC's 143, 110, 167. Supt Insp Johns No flows, Nill viz and thick mud.
17/1/88 ②	Stoney Cove Leicestershire (BSAC)	Dive at Stoney Cove carrying out Advanced Diver Safety & Rescue skills. This included remove mask refit clear twice, remove DV, recover, twice shore DV as recover & doner. bouyant lift EAR on surface. and 50 mtr tow giving EAR. Pos Jetstream used.
21/1/88 ③	Woolwich Aquatic Centre	Pleasure dive good viz. practise drills test value

| TIMES | | | | Max Depth Metres | Remarks | Signatures of (a) Diver (b) Supervisor |
Left Surface	Left Bottom	Bottom Time	Reached Surface			
1030		55	1125	1·5	No trace Weapons prev found. Not to continue.	(a) *[signature]* (b) *[signature]*
		25.		21	Neil Webb used as body for test. ivor cold fantastic viz. DO Martin Smith Exam Inst.	(a) *[signature]* (b) *[signature]* CISCO3.
1600		55	1655	8	Cold Water good viz	(a) *[signature]*

Date	Location	Details of Operation
23/1/88 (4)	River Lea Navigation Lea Bridge Road, E.5	Search for shotgun, sawn off. Aga used. Stby 114, Attendants 97, 110, 143, 167. Supv 110 Nil viz 2 knot flow stoney Bottom. Cold water hands frozen after 50 mins no feel. Shivering. 15 25
30/1/88 (5)	Regents Canal. Aberdeen Road / Cunningham Place.	Search for High Value Watches Aga used Stby 110 Attds 97 143, 146, Supervisor P&24 6" to 12" viz slight flow leafy bottom with usual rubbish
8/2/88 (6)	River Lea Lea Bridge Road	Search for shotgun. sawn off. Aga used. Stby 110. Attds 114 113, 146 Super Insp Johns. Stony Bottom. Cold water 1 knot flow

TIMES				Max Depth Metres	Remarks	Signatures of (a) Diver (b) Supervisor
Left Surface	Left Bottom	Bottom Time	Reached Surface			
1020		50	1110	2.4	No further to Continue	(a) [signature]
					CIBZ investigate re. poss suicide	
						(b) [signature]
					for DM . CID	(a) [signature]
1010		50	1100	3		
						(b) [signature] P524
1035		55	1130	2.4		
					CIBZ Investigation	(a) [signature]

Date	Location	Details of Operation
16/2/88 ⑦⑧	St Catherines Dock London E.1.	Search for broken mooring chains on pontoon. Jackstay search. Aga used. Stby 146, Attds 97, 144, Supt PS24 Broken vil viz. 2ft thick mud.
1/3/88 ⑨	ALBERT DOCK 21 shed.	Search for Drugs. Jackstay search, Aga used Stby 146, Attds 144, 198. Supr. PS24. mud/silt bottom Water bloody cold. 1ft/nil viz
10/3/88 ⑩	Woolwich Aquatic Centre	Dive buddied to Dyk Hinson, SMB used 8ft viz Aga used Attds 130, Insp Johns Supr Insp John

TIMES				Max Depth Metres	Remarks	Signatures of (a) Diver (b) Supervisor
Left Surface	Left Bottom	Bottom Time	Reached Surface			
1020		20	1040	6·7	Chain	(a) [signature]
1110		10	1120	6·7	Recovered and buoyed for joining later.	(b) [signature] Pozu
1200		50	1250	10·3	No trace to Continue	(a) [signature] (b) [signature] Pozu
1120		29	1210	8·3	Routine Transit.	(a) [signature] (b) [signature]

Date	Location	Details of Operation
23/3/88 (11)	Regents Canal Commercial Road Bridge	Search for head and torso / Possibly seperated. Against Stoky 97, Attds 110,114,144 146, Supervisor 24, N.11 viz slight flow. bottom full of rubbish & thick mud.
1/4/88 (12)	Fort Bovisand Harbour Plymouth (BSAC)	Dive with Hawkins good viz some ... Pat Maxwell used. rocky bottoms. D.H. Alan Vick
2/4/88 (13)	Gweal-Mewstone of Fort Bovisand. (BSAC)	Dive with Cavan Spelbury good viz rocky, kelp. caught a nice crab. Poss Maxwell used. Dive Marshall Dane Spelbury -

TIMES				Max Depth Metres	Remarks	Signatures of (a) Diver (b) Supervisor
Left Surface	Left Bottom	Bottom Time	Reached Surface			
1010		50	1100	3	No time to Continue	(a) *[signature]* (b) *[signature]* 524
1410		60	1510	7.1	Good buddy Kept close throughout dive, clear signals.	(a) *[signature]* (b)
1128		27	1157	10	Good buddy. Kept close. throughout. Had problem with weight	(a) *[signature]* (b) *[signature]* Bradbury

Date	Location	Details of Operation
2/4/88 (14)	Breakwater Plymouth Sound	Dive with Jason Vick Novice Diver on the outside of breakwater. Divers Knife found. Good viz large rocks on bottom. Poss used. DM. Dave Screenhawy.
3/4/88 (15)	U.S.S. Wreck James Eagun Layne built 1944 Whitsand Bay Cornwall. Sunk 24/3/1945 by a U Boat	Dive with Loraine Cook. on her first wreck. trouble with ears at first but cleared after descent. Poss used. Water clear slight flow (springs). Lots of large fish
4/4/88 (16)	Dive on the Fort. near Plymouth Sound Breakwater	Dive with Jean Stone, lots of Rubbish about. occasional nil viz due to stirring up fine sand. Poss Used. Springs Saw one large Ray

<table>
<tr><td colspan="4">TIMES</td><td>Max
Depth
Metres</td><td>Remarks</td><td>Signatures of
(a) Diver
(b) Supervisor</td></tr>
<tr><td>Left
Surface</td><td>Left
Bottom</td><td>Bottom
Time</td><td>Reached
Surface</td><td></td><td></td><td></td></tr>
<tr><td>1725</td><td></td><td>30</td><td>1755</td><td>13</td><td>Good dive, Rebecca.
Kept close
used new.
Dry suit,</td><td>(a) [signature]

(b) [signature]</td></tr>
<tr><td></td><td></td><td>33.</td><td></td><td>19.2.</td><td>Lorraine is
now a very
competent diver
and seems to
be more relaxed.
I enjoy diving
with her.</td><td>(a) [signature]

(b) [signature]</td></tr>
<tr><td>1547</td><td></td><td>39</td><td>1626</td><td>13.1</td><td>Jean good
diver kept
close.</td><td>(a) [signature]

(b) [signature]</td></tr>
</table>

Date	Location	Details of Operation
5/1/88 (17) (18)	EIK Reef – off Plymouth Sound	Dive with Richard and Steve Chambers on a beautifull reef. Lots of [illegible] coral and sea [illegible]. Rocky bottom viz about 40 ft slight flow. Pan used. Dive Marshall Sve Daw. (1st dive bounce to see if [illegible]
6/1/88 (19)	Dive and Shagstone and wreck.	Dive with Matthew Freeman and Barry Chambers on Shagstone. Found wreck. good viz 20 ft. lots of kelp. Pan used. Dive marshall.
7/1/88 (20)	Dive on wreck James Eagin Layne off Whitsand Bay Cornwall	Dive with Steve Chambers on this wreck, went inside lots of fish. Pan used. Dive Marshall.

TIMES				Max Depth Metres	Remarks	Signatures of (a) Diver (b) Supervisor
Left Surface	Left Bottom	Bottom Time	Reached Surface			
1427		4	1431	27	Steve chamber	
1345		16	1401	31	good & confident	
					Diver. Richard	
					was apprehensive	
					prior to dive (b)	
					but OK when	
					on bottom	
1028		42	1107	46	Matt good diver	(a)
					and stayed. Bonny	D Chenb
					too fast apt	
					to fly aft. OK (b)	
					after corrected	
0955		36	0231		Steve good	(a)
					diver is safe	
					at all times	
						(b) J Clark

Date	Location	Details of Operation
7/4/88 (21)	Dive at Chadwell Spring Range Hd. Below church on Hill. Boreshal	Dive with Steve Chambers. Went crab hunting. Lots of small ones not large enough to eat but nice dive good viz. Lots of work & kelp Poss used. Dive Manbul Matt Freeman.
22/4/88 (22)	Grand Union Canal Bulls Bridge Southall	Dive for two Cash boxes within Robbery. Aga used Stilby 143 Mtbs. 114, 143, 130 Super 24. Nil Viz. no flow.
3/5/88 (23)	River Thames under Grosvenor Rail Bridge	Dive for Knife used in Murder on Train. Aga used. 3 Knots flow 2 inch viz. Stilby 143, Mtbs 97 130 Super 24.

TIMES				Max Depth Metres	Remarks	Signatures of (a) Diver (b) Supervisor
Left Surface	Left Bottom	Bottom Time	Reached Surface			
1730		48	1818	9		(a)
						(b)
11∞		20	1120	3	Two cash Boxes recovered statement — given to CID at 'TW'	(a) (b)
1120		40	1200	4	N/s to Continue	(a) (b)

Date	Location	Details of Operation
5/5/88 (24)	Grand Union Canal Danbury St N1. Frog Lane Bridge	Search for Hand Guns. Aga used. Attds 97 114 130 Super 24. Slight flow N1 V13.
18/5/88 (25)	Search for Car in River Thames 300 yds Upstream from Walton Bridge Shepperton	Search for Car Aga used Attds. 146 143 198 St Ley 130 Nil Wave Super 24 Slight flow 1ft V13 torch used
29/5/88 (26)	[illegible] North Salcombe Haven (BSAC) [illegible]	Dive with Very Hammond Kt open water dive in the water [illegible] Kit used 10ft V13 shingle bottom.

TIMES				Max Depth Metres	Remarks	Signatures of (a) Diver (b) Supervisor
Left Surface	Left Bottom	Bottom Time	Reached Surface			
1205		30	1235	2·4	No time to Continue	(a) [signature] (b) [signature] J24
1100 ~~1200~~		60	1200	4·2	Can [_____] opened [_____] ok.	(a) [signature] (b) [signature] J24
1540		35	1615	8	good diver confident — [_____] [illegible]	(a) [signature] (b)

Date	Location	Details of Operation
30/5/88 (27)	Hallsands North Salcombe Devon (BSAC)	Beach dive on reef West of North Hallsands Beach. Aqua Lung used also used Wetsuit for first time in UK. Waters good viz, rocky bottom. Buddy Joe Jackson.
(28)	Chelsea Bridge River Thames	Dive for gold. Aqua was Nil viz. [illegible] 97 198 8 key 144 Super 143. 3 Knot flow nil viz.
5/6/88 (29)	Dive on wreck Bazill off Littlehampton (BSAC)	Dive with Dave Spenbury on wreck Bazill. Poss used good viz although dark, torch used, saw large fish and shells. Hardboat dive –

TIMES				Max Depth Metres	Remarks	Signatures of (a) Diver (b) Supervisor
Left Surface	Left Bottom	Bottom Time	Reached Surface			
1213		56	1309	10	Enjoyable Dive got 8 crabs inc an giant & Spider crab.	(a) [signature] (b)
					Old shirkly fw legs [illegible]	(a) [signature]
[illegible] 1000		[illegible]	0085	34		(b) [signature]
9.46		10	9.56	37		(a) [signature] (b) D A Speedo C12826.

Date	Location	Details of Operation
5/6/88 (30)	Dive on reef in Sea off Littlehampton (BSAC)	Dive with Tony Smith & Simon Steadman on reef. Pair used 10ft viz slight flow got dogfish not very tasty
19/6/88 (31)	River Thames Upriver from Westminster Bridge.	Dive on m/v Interceptor re possible fouled screw. Viga used. Stby 9t. AHoc 130, Incap J. Super Incap J. 3 knot flow nil viz.
4/6/88 (32)	Dive in sewer. Fish Pond.	Search for pike ord. Pair used nil viz AH depth PC 146 Super PS Brooks. Water cold

TIMES				Max Depth Metres	Remarks	Signatures of (a) Diver (b) Supervisor
Left Surface	Left Bottom	Bottom Time	Reached Surface			
		7		14		(a) [signature]
					(b)
1205	20-	1225.	2	Plastic wrapped around one prop. rope on other prop. cleared with. knife.	(a) McLauchlan (b) [signature]
1100		1201	8.4	Various Ports and. plus folded chair handed to Manager of SEVAC.	(a) McLauchlan (b) [signature]

Date	Location	Details of Operation
8/7/88 (33)	River Thames Kingston Bridge	Search for Hammer used in murder and blood saturated curtains in plastic carry bag. Agg used. Stby 99, Athd 114 144 Supv. Insp J. Slight flow. 12" viz rocky bottom as usual - change!
13ᵗʰ/88 (34)	River Thames Hammersmith Bridge	Search for suit-case size package. Pass/ Ex026 marks used. 1ft viz 3 Knot current. Including search. Stby. 114 Athd 144, 24, 146. Supv Insp J. Strong Bottom
(35)	Lake, Thurrock Angling club Warwick Lane Rainham.	Search for hatchet used in murder. pluss hands and head (poss) Ex026 used. Supv 24, Stby 98. Nil viz. muddy bottom.

TIMES				Max Depth Metres	Remarks	Signatures of (a) Diver (b) Supervisor
Left Surface	Left Bottom	Bottom Time	Reached Surface			
1125		55	1220	4	N/T to Continue	(a) _[signature]_
						(b) _[signature]_
1210		:20	1230	2	N/T to Continue.	(a) _[signature]_
						(b) _[signature]_
1030		60	1130	3	N.T viz. found shotguns and saw. handed to KB CID.	(a) _[signature]_ (b) _[signature]_

Date	Location	Details of Operation
18/7/88 (36)	Thurrock Angling Club. Rainham.	Search for Axe used in murder. Aqua used. Stby 144 Attds. 198 - 95. Supv Insp. Nil viz. thick mud.
10/8/88 (37)	Royal Vic Dock Canning Town London.	Search for sunken Boat, tent poles and Parachute. Aqua used Stby .114. Attds 143 130 Supv 143. Nil viz thick black mud on bottom.
15/8/88 (38)	River Thames Tower Bridge.	Dive for bag cont Shotgun & Pistol. Aqua used, Stdby .144 Amos Attds 143, 94, 84. Supv 24. Nil viz 2 knot flow. Jackstay Search

TIMES				Max Depth Metres	Remarks	Signatures of (a) Diver (b) Supervisor
Left Surface	Left Bottom	Bottom Time	Reached Surface			
1130		40	1210	2	N/T to Continue.	(a) [signature]
						(b) [signature]
1000		44	1044	10	Boat found one pole found. on surfacing burst blood vesel in sinus. blood nose / mouth.	(a) [signature] (b) Arnold [signature] 163
1100		50	1130	4	N/T to Continue.	(a) [signature] (b)

Date	Location	Details of Operation
8/9/88 (39)	West India Dock Marsh Wall London	Search for £5,000 Computer. Swim. Aga used. Stilley 130, Atteb 24, 146, Super 24. N.l viz.
11/9/88 (40)	River Thames. Festival Pier	Security search. Aga used Stilley 198 Atteb 130, 146, 143 Super hosp J. N.l viz Sharp flow.
29/9/88 (41)	SHARM / EL / SHEIKH RED SEA. OFF LARGE M.V COLOUR IV	Dive with Vicky Harwood in clear blue water viz. forever. fish seen: Lion Fish, Napolean Wrasse, Scorpion Fish, Parrot fish Black chest Butterfly, Goldenstriped grouper loss used. wet suit

TIMES				Max Depth Metres	Remarks	Signatures of (a) Diver (b) Supervisor
Left Surface	Left Bottom	Bottom Time	Reached Surface			
						(a)
1100		45	1145	10	Seen found and returned to owner.	
						(b)
0945		75	1100	4	Cleaned and left sterile	(a)
						(b)
0910		33	0943	12	Club Bottom rubbish but lots of fish	(a)
						(b)

Date	Location	Details of Operation
29/9/88 (42)	FISHERMANS BANK · RED SEA · (Colona IV) ·	Dive with King Howard. Clear Blue Water, slight flow. Wall reef. saw turtle 3 white tip sharks. 2 black tip sharks lots of other fish incl. large Napolean wrass. Poss. wreck. Dive from Inflatable
29/9/88 (43)	REEF CALLED ALTERNATIVES ABOUT 20 MILES SOUTH RAS MOHAMMED RED SEA (night-Dive) (Colona IV)	Dive with Steve Wilkie on night dive on reef. lots of fish including lion fish large parrot fish parrot wrass slight flow.

TIMES				Max Depth Metres	Remarks	Signatures of (a) Diver (b) Supervisor
Left Surface	Left Bottom	Bottom Time	Reached Surface			
1345		57.	1442	13	Very pretty with bonny coral reef. spectacular. long swim back to boat	(a) [signature] (b) [signature]
1845.		45.	1950	11	Torch worked well strange feeling and dissorientation	(a) [signature] (b)

Date	Location	Details of Operation
30/9/88 (44)	DIVE ON SHARM REEF RAS MOHAMED. RED SEA (Colora IV)	Dive with Kay on this wall reef that goes down forever. saw large Napoleon wrasse school of barracuda, school of shark and every concievable type of fish in the red sea. it was so mind blowing. pom went
30/9/88 (45)	TEMPLE JUST DOWN FROM SHARM REEF DIVE RED SEA (Colara II)	Dive with Kay on a lovely reef. Saw lots of fish. fed Napoleon wrasse with bread. agreyable perfect viz

TIMES				Max Depth Metres	Remarks	Signatures of (a) Diver (b) Supervisor
Left Surface	Left Bottom	Bottom Time	Reached Surface			
0925		30	0955	16	Swam against current on one side of reef, and drifted on the other like a man in space had to come up Kenyons 40 bar.	(a) [signature] (b) [signature]
1542		34	1616	18	mouthpiece split, breath half water and air, changed to Air II ok but made jaw ache.	(a) [signature] (b) [signature]

Date	Location	Details of Operation
3/9/88 (46)	TEMPLE JUST DOWN FROM SHARM, REEF DIVE, NIGH DIVE (Colona II)	Dive with Vaxy Hammond on night dive on good reef, saw lots of fish. Many fish. Torch good. Poss used.
31/10/88 (47)	BEACON ROCK RED SEA. (Colona II) Wreck Dive. 'DUNRAVEN'	Left Colona II in inflatable for wreck Dunraven. Dived with Vaxy, entered wreck with torch, saw many large groupers and lion fish. Poss used, slight flow incread vis.
1/10/88 (48)	BEACON ROCK RED SEA (Colona II) reef dive	Dive with dave Willie usual fish except for Blue Spotted Stingray, looked lovely, strong flow. Comp Nav to boat Poss used.

TIMES				Max Depth Metres	Remarks	Signatures of (a) Diver (b) Supervisor
Left Surface	Left Bottom	Bottom Time	Reached Surface			
1845.		37	1922	12.4	Good nav in deinle also stake an ladder	(a) [signature] (b) [signature]
1030		29.	1056	26	Dive to 26 mts. far 24 mins. then to 6 mts. far 5 min.	(a) [signature] (b) [signature]
1520		24	1544	15	Dive to 24	(a) [signature]
1544		11	1555	6m	with Decom at 6m for 11 min.	(b)

Date	Location	Details of Operation
31/10/88 (49)	BEACON ROCK RED SEA (Colona II) Night dive.	Dive with Steve Wilkie ourself. saw barracuda Spanish Dancer; small eel. compass nav back to boat. Poss used.
2/10/88 (50)	RAS MOHAMED SOUTH ISLAND RED SEA	Dive with Kay. fought a strong current from boat to reef. Had some bread in plastic bag. large Napoleon wrasse about 10ft in dia surged by and all the bread away from me. I was amazed how strong he was. drifted back on current to boat. Poss used.

TIMES				Max Depth Metres	Remarks	Signatures of (a) Diver (b) Supervisor
Left Surface	Left Bottom	Bottom Time	Reached Surface			
						(a)
1820		44	1906	12	Dive to 12	
1906		2	1908	6	meter then	
					to 6m for	
					2 min decom (b)	
1035		34	1109	20	Strong current a	
					used most	
					of air got	
					stung big	
					fire coral	
					was very (b)	
					tired	

Date	Location	Details of Operation
2/10/88 (51)	ANEMNOME CITY RAS MOHAMED RED SEA. (CORONA II)	Dive with Steve Wilkie on a beautifull cliff. Soon as we started to descend we saw a large turtle. the the usual Napoleon vass then seen to follow divers everywhere viz fantastic sea a bit ruff. Poss used.
2/10/88 (52)	TEMPLE Red Sea. Night Dive (Corona).	Dive with Keny an reef. Renzo boat skipper took camera and made a video of dive. fantastic scorpion fish, lion fish. Blue angle fish large fan coral, just to good to explain unless you are there. Poss used. no flaw very dark

TIMES				Max Depth Metres	Remarks	Signatures of (a) Diver (b) Supervisor
Left Surface	Left Bottom	Bottom Time	Reached Surface			
1450		20	1530	15		(a)
1510			1530	6 m		
						(v)
1830		38	1908	13	Strike put on bottom of boat ladder	(a)
						(b)

Date	Location	Details of Operation
3/10/88 (53)	RAS EL SID NEAR TEMPLE RED SEA.	Dive with Kay on Wall reef, this dive followed a snorkle where we saw three bf sharks it was good. In the dive we saw a fantastic napolian wrass and all fed it with boiled eggs this was being filmed by Renza so we have something to show how fantastic the Red sea is for fish life and divers. This is the last dive on the Colona II and it was a dive to end a perfect week afloat and diving. Poss usd

TIMES				Max Depth Metres	Remarks	Signatures of (a) Diver (b) Supervisor
Left Surface	Left Bottom	Bottom Time	Reached Surface			
1020		24	1054	27		(a)
1044		10	1054	6		
				surface 1055		
						(b)

Date	Location	Details of Operation
5/10/88 (54)	Shore Dive · Gulf of Eilat Isreal.	Shore Dive with Keny. measured small Coral clusters good viz — pen used feel As
5/10/88 (55)	Shore Dive Gulf of Eilat - Isreal.	Dive with Keny down slope past coral clusters, loss of colou Raptur noticable in breathing
4/10/88 (56)	Shore Dive gulf Eilat - Isreal.	Dive with Keny, drove air at 40m. Keny confident at depth loss of colours.
6/10/88 (57)	Shore Dive Gulf Eilat Isreal.	Dive with Keny bread for fish saw five lion fish moray eel lots more
7/10/88 (58)	Shore Dive Isreal.	Dive with Keny. slipped n inj knee Played with fish
7/10/88 (59)	Shore Dive Gulf at Eilat	Dive with keny took Bred to feed fish .
8/10/88 (69)	Shore Dive Gulf at Eilat	Dive with keny on depth Training exercise

TIMES				Max Depth Metres	Remarks	Signatures of (a) Diver (b) Supervisor
Left Surface	Left Bottom	Bottom Time	Reached Surface			
1000	1034	35	1045	30	Table (a)	(a) _signature_
1039		10	1045	6	Decom at 6m B/T Surface	
					to 6m then 6m for 10 min	
1510	1520	23	1538	45	Table c	(a) _signature_
1523		2	1538	9	Decom 2min	
1526		12	1538	6	Decom 12min	
1015	1028	17	1043	48	1min at	_signature_
1031		1	1032	9	9 mins	
1032		10	1043		10min at 6m	
1520		55	1616	9	Table C	(a) _signature_
1010	1036	37	1106	21	Table (a)	(a) _signature_
1037		29	1106	6		
1610	1631	22	1645	23	Table c	(a) _signature_
1632		13	1645	6		
1020	1030	19	1056	50	Table 'A'	
1039		2	.	9		

DATE	COURSES — QUALIFICATIONS — SPECIAL EXPERIENCE
21/5/84 to 13/7/84.	Basic Diving Course at the Police National Diving School. Northumbria Police, North Dock Sunderland
2ND. SEP. 85. UNTIL. 13TH. SEP. 85.	ATTEND REFRESHER DIVING COURSE AT NATIONAL POLICE DIVING SCHOOL. NORTHUMBRIA POLICE, NORTH DOCK. SUNDERLAND

DATE	COURSES — QUALIFICATIONS — SPECIAL EXPERIENCE
17·11·86 | 5·12·86	ATTENDED AND SUCCESSFULLY COMPLETED A SUPERVISORS COURSE AT THE NATIONAL POLICE DIVING SCHOOL, SUNDERLAND.

NORTHUMBRIA
POLICE
5 DEC 1986
NATIONAL POLICE
DIVING SCHOOL

DATE	COURSES — QUALIFICATIONS — SPECIAL EXPERIENCE

MEDICAL CERTIFICATE

Full name of Diver: .....MACKENZIE WILLIAM MOULTON.....

Date of Medical Examination: .....10/1/84.....

Date of X Ray Examination: .....14/12/83.....

Result of Medical Examination—FIT/UNFIT: .....

Medical Restriction on Diving (if applicable):

.....

..... None .....

.....

.....

.....

.....

Duration of Validity of Certificate:

..... 1 year. .....

Name of Approved Doctor: ..... Dr J. MINNIS .....

Address of Approved Doctor: ..... St George's Lodge
The Burroughs Hendon N.W.4

Telephone number of Approved Doctor: ..... 202-6232 .....

Signature of Approved Doctor: .....

Met. Police
Medical Centre
Aerodrome Road
London NW9 5JE

MEDICAL NOTE

Blood Group ....

....

Sickle Cell Test: .... 10/11/84 .... Named ....

....

Any Allergies: .... No ....

....

....

....

....

....

Any other points which would be of assistance in an emergency:

....

.... None. ....

....

....

....

....

....

....

....

....

MEDICAL CERTIFICATE

Full name of Diver: *Mackenzie William MOULTON*

Date of Medical Examination: *7-8-85*

Date of X Ray Examination: *11-7-85*

Result of Medical Examination—FIT/UNFIT: *Ref N⁰ 08346*

Medical Restriction on Diving (if applicable):

NONE

Duration of Validity of Certificate: *1 year*

Name of Approved Doctor: *N. J. MINNIS*   Met. Police Medical Centre

Address of Approved Doctor: Aerodrome Road London NW9 5JE

Telephone number of Approved Doctor: *202-6232*

Signature of Approved Doctor:

MEDICAL CERTIFICATE

Full name of Diver: ...... MacKenzie William MOULTON ......

Date of Medical Examination: ...... 5/8/87 ......

Date of X Ray Examination: ...... 21/7/87 ......

Result of Medical Examination—FIT/UNFIT: ...... Ref No 29097 ......

Medical Restriction on Diving (if applicable):

...... None ......

....

....

....

....

....

Duration of Validity of Certificate:

...... 1 year ......

Name of Approved Doctor: ...... J. MINNIS ......

Address of Approved Doctor: ...... Met Police Medical Centre
...... Aerodrome Rd. N.W.9. ......

Telephone number of Approved Doctor: ...... 202 - 6232 ......

Signature of Approved Doctor: ...... J. Minnis MR ......

That is the end of my first Police Divers logbook. There are two more, but I will only be publishing the second one as the last only contained a few dives before I retired and was seized by CIB2, thats an internal investigation branch of The Metropolitan Police and another story.

As you can see by reading my Police Divers logbook, I have done a lot of leisure diving and to do this I had to join the BSAC.

Despite being highly qualified and having a commercial HSE divers certificate and qualified as a Diving Operations Supervisor, they insisted I do further training to acquire my Advanced Diver qualifications, and in the next few pages I have included

copies of my BSAC qualifications
obtained for your viewing.

BRITISH SUB-AQUA CLUB

16 Upper Woburn Place, London WC1H 0QW
Telephone: 01-387 9302

Details of Member

Surname MOULTON

Forenames MACKENZIE.

Membership No. 3 4 4 9 2 1

Home Address

(work) 98, WAPPING HIGH
ST. LONDON. E·1·

Telephone 01- 488 -5096/5095

Date of Birth 21 - 6 - 1947

Blood Group
(If known)

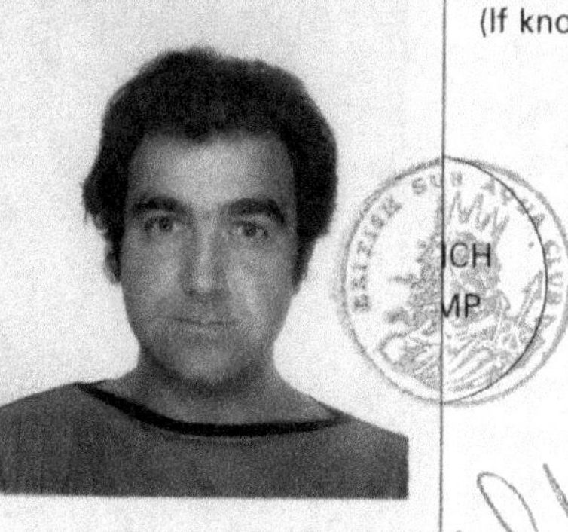

Signature of Member

If found, please return this logbook to member or Club HQ.

DETAILS OF MEMBER'S BRANCH

LOGBOOK ISSUED BY

Name of Branch: BEXLEY

Branch Number: 982   Date of Issue: 1-7-86

Change of Branch, to: 108 RICHMOND.

Branch Number: 108   Date of Change: 1 FEB 89.

Change of Branch, to:

Branch Number: Date of Change:

SUMMARY OF QUALIFICATIONS GAINED
(Enter date awarded)

Novice Diver	1-7-86	(page 11)
Sports Diver	1-7-86.	(page 15)
Dive Leader	20-1-87	(page 19)
Advanced Diver	9-2-88	(page 23)
First Class Diver		(page 24)
Club Instructor		(page 26)
Advanced Instructor		(page 27)
National Instructor		(page 28)

NOVICE DIVER TRAINING RECORD

Subject Code	Description of Training	Date	Instructor's Signature (No. if relevant)
	Introduction to Diving Course		
	Swimming Ability Check— 100m freestyle	July 84	
	Satisfactory Medical Examination and X-Ray (page 5)		
NT1	*Theory Lesson:* Introduction to Branch and Diver Training		
NT2	*Theory Lesson:* Basic Equipment		
NT3	*Theory Lesson:* Signals	H.S.E. PART III	C13103
NT4	*Theory Lesson:* Causes and Effects of Pressure		
NS1	*Practical Skill Group:* Using Mask, Fins and Snorkel		
NT5	*Theory Lesson:* Aqualung Breathing Apparatus		
NS2	*Practical Skill Group:* Aqualung Skills—Group 1		

Subject Code	Description of Training	Date	Instructor's Signature (No. if relevant)
NT6	*Theory Lesson:* The Human Life-Support System		
NS3	*Practical Skill Group:* Breath-hold Diving	July 84	
NS4	*Practical Skill Group:* Aqualung Skills—Group 2		
NS5	*Practical Skill Group:* Aqualung Skills—Group 3		
BASIC SKILLS TEST	Part 1	H.S.E. PART III	C13103
	Part 2		
NT7	*Theory Lesson:* Buoyancy Devices		
NS6	*Practical Skill Group:* ABLJ/BC Skills		
NT8	*Theory Lesson:* Diver Rescue—Part 1		
NS7	*Practical Skill Group:* Rescue Skills—Group 1		
NT9	*Theory Lesson:* Safe Diving Practices		

Subject Code	Description of Training	Date	Instructor's Signature (No. if relevant)
ABLJ/BC AND RESCUE SKILLS TEST		July 84	
NT10	*Theory Lesson:* Diving Suits & Accessories		
NT11	*Theory Lesson:* Equipment Care & Storage	H.S.E. PART III	C13103
NT12	*Theory Lesson:* Dry Suit Diving		
NS8	*Practical Skill Group:* Full Equipment Familiarisation		
FULL EQUIPMENT TEST			
NT13	*Theory Lesson:* Where to Dive, What to Do		

THEORY TEST

Date successfully completed	Branch Diving Officer
	C13103

NOVICE DIVER QUALIFICATION

A diver who is ready to gain open water diving experience in the company of a Dive Leader or higher qualified Diver/Instructor, being competent in the safe and correct use of all appropriate open water aqualung diving equipment in a sheltered water training area.

This is to certify that

MACKENZIE MOULTON

has completed the required training and is ready to embark on open water dives as a

BSAC NOVICE DIVER

C13103

Branch Diving Officer

Branch Secretary

1 – 7 – 86

Date

(Equivalent to CMAS One Star Diver)

SPORTS DIVER TRAINING RECORD

Subject Code	Description of Training	Date	Instructor's Signature (No. if relevant)
ST1	*Theory Lesson:* Diver Rescue—Part 2		
SS1	*Practical Skill Group:* Rescue Skills—Group 2		

Ideally, the Rescue Training above should be completed before any open water qualifying dives are undertaken.

Skill and Confidence Building Exercises, and the following required training, may take place concurrently with qualifying dives.

Subject Code	Description of Training	Date	Instructor's Signature (No. if relevant)
ST2	*Theory Lesson:* Diving from Boats		
ST3	*Theory Lesson:* Underwater Navigation		
SS2	*Open Water Lesson:* Underwater Navigation		
ST4	*Theory Lesson:* N_2 Absorption: Gas Toxicity		
ST5	*Theory Lesson:* Deep Diving		

SPORTS DIVER TRAINING RECORD

Subject Code	Description of Training	Date	Instructor's Signature (No. if relevant)
ST6	*Theory Lesson:* Decompression Tables		
ST7	*Theory Lesson:* Air Requirements		
SS3	*Open Water Lesson:* Using Surface Marker Buoy		
ST8	*Theory Lesson:* Arranging Your Own Dives		
ST9	*Theory Lesson:* Diving Safety Review		
OPEN WATER—SAFETY AND RESCUE SKILLS TEST			

THEORY TEST

Date successfully completed	Branch Diving Officer
	C 13103

SPORTS DIVER QUALIFYING DIVES

10 open water dives to be completed from at least 5 different sites and on at least 5 different dates. Each dive to have a minimum submerged duration of 15 minutes; Total duration of the 10 dives to be not less than 5 hours. Dives should show experience of any 5 of the following:— Shore dive/Small boat dive/Fresh water dive/Moving water (1 kt) dive/Sea water dive/Limited visibility dive (approximately 2 m)/Cold water dive (less than 10°C)/Dive to 25m.

Member to read notes on page 4 before recording dives here.

Type of Qualifying Dive	Date	Site	Dive details verified by
		H.S.E PART III	

CERTIFICATION OF QUALIFYING DIVES

C 13103 ... Date 1-7-86

Branch Diving Officer

STATEMENT OF ALTERNATIVE TRAINING

The holder of this logbook

MACKENZIE MOULTON

(Name)

has obtained the

H.S.E. PART III (CERT. No. 561/84)

(Title of Qualification)

issued by

HEALTH AND SAFETY EXECUTIVE

(Name of Agency/Federation)

This qualification has a CMAS TWO STAR rating.

The BSAC National Diving Officer considers this qualification to be of a similar standard to

BSAC SPORTS DIVER, grade

and the holder may therefore begin training for the next higher BSAC Qualification.

C 13103

Diving Officer

1-7-86

Date

DIVER LEADER TRAINING RECORD

Subject Code	Description of Training	Date	Instructor's Signature (No. if relevant)
LT1	Theory Lesson: Dive Leadership	6-3-87	*signature* C13432
LT2	Theory Lesson: Adventurous Diving	4/2/87	M Collins AI 87
LT3	Theory Lesson: Diver Rescue—Part 3	6-3-87	*signature* C13432
LT4	Theory Lesson: Charts, Tides, Weather—Part 1	9/12/86	M Collins AI 87
LT5	Theory Lesson: Recognition of Diving Disorders	16/12/86	*signature* Broadbury
LT6	Theory Lesson: Decompression Tables and Air Requirements Review	30/1/87	*signature* C13103

DIVE LEADER TRAINING RECORD

Description of Training	Date	Instructor's Signature (No. if relevant)
OPEN WATER DIVE LEADERSHIP—ASSESSMENT DIVE 1	4 MAR 87	*signature* C13432
OPEN WATER DIVE LEADERSHIP—ASSESSMENT DIVE 2	4 MAR 87	*signature* C13432
OPEN WATER DIVE LEADERSHIP—ASSESSMENT DIVE 3	26/10/86	A F Smith C12847.
OPEN WATER—SAFETY AND RESCUE SKILLS TEST	26/10/86	A F Smith C12847.

THEORY TEST

Date successfully completed	Branch Diving Officer
20/1/87	*signature* C13.103

DIVE LEADER QUALIFYING DIVES

10 open water dives to be completed from at least 5 different sites and on at least 5 different dates. Each dive to have a minimum submerged duration of 15 minutes: Total duration of the 10 dives to be not less than 5 hours. Dives should show experience of any 4 of the following:— Large boat dive/Wreck dive/Drift dive/Dive to 35 m/ Dive with simulated decompression stops/Cold water: cold weather dive (less than 5°C)/Low visibility dive (less than 1 m).

Member to read notes on page 4 before recording dives here.

Type of Qualifying Dive	Date	Site	Dive details verified by
(1) Drift Dive	6/7/1986	SEA SHOREHAM	
(2) Water Rescue etc.	21/10/86	(Qual Div 10) GILDENBURGH WATER.	
(3) Fresh Water D/C Procedure	4/3/87	(Qual Div 9) LUXBOROUGH LAKE	
(4) Fresh Water Nil Viz	4/3/87	LUXBOROUGH LAKE	
(5) Cold Water Dive	22/3/87	STONEY COVE	
(6) Sea Dive Buoyancy BSD/L	10/5/87	SEAFORD	
(7) Sea Wreck Dive	24/5/87	THURLSTON SANDS SALCOMBE DEVON	
(8) Deep Dive on Wreck	25/5/87	CHALLABOROUGH BIGBURY BAY DEVON	
(9) Sea Dive on Wreck	27/5/87	HOPE COVE SALCOMBE DEVON	
(10) Sea Dive on Wreck	28/5/87	STAIR HOLE BAY SOUTH SAND DEVON	

CERTIFICATION OF QUALIFYING DIVES

30 — 6 — 87   *signature* C13103
Date
Branch Diving Officer

DIVE LEADER QUALIFICATION

An active, experienced and responsible diver, competent in dive leadership, who may lead Novice and Sports Divers on open water dives.

This is to certify that

MACKENZIE MOULTON

has completed the required training
and is qualified to attend
open water meetings as a

BSAC DIVE LEADER

signature C13103
Branch Diving Officer

Susan E Dow
Branch Secretary

6-7-1987
Date

★ ★

(Equivalent to CMAS Two Star Diver)

BSAC SKILL DEVELOPMENT COURSES

ALTERNATIVE TRAINING

M W MOULTON

has completed a course in

UNDERWATER PHOTOGRAPHY

run by

NORTHUMBRIA POLICE

BSAC considers that this training achieves
the same objectives as the BSAC Skill
Development Course in

UNDERWATER PHOTOGRAPHY

and will accept it accordingly

Verified

27.8.92

Date

Robin Eccles
Coaching Manager

Verified by

Robin Eccles
Coaching Manager

MARINE RADIO OPERATION

BSAC SKILL DEVELOPMENT COURSES

ALTERNATIVE TRAINING

M W MOULTON

has completed a course in

NAVIGATION

run by

ROYAL YACHTING ASSOCIATION

BSAC considers that this training achieves
the same objectives as the BSAC Skill
Development Course in

NAVIGATION

and will accept it accordingly

Verified

27.8.92

Date

Robin Eccles
Coaching Manager

BRITISH SUB-AQUA CLUB

M W MOULTON

has completed RYA training which
exceeds the requirements of the
BSAC CHARTWORK Course

Verified by

Robin Eccles
Coaching Manager

CHARTWORK

THE BRITISH SUB-AQUA CLUB

M W MOULTON

holds the Restricted Certificate of
Competence in RADIO TELEGRAPHY

Certificate No: MT/11372

Verified by

Robin Eccles
Coaching Manager

MARINE RADIO OPERATION

BSAC SKILL DEVELOPMENT COURSES

ALTERNATIVE TRAINING

M W MOULTON

has completed a course in

RECOVERY & LIFTING

run by

NORTHUMBRIA POLICE

BSAC considers that this training achieves
the same objectives as the BSAC Skill
Development Course in

RECOVERY & LIFTING

and will accept it accordingly

Verified

27.8.92

Date

DEVELOPMENT COURSES

ALTERNATIVE TRAINING

M W MOULTON

has completed a course in

COMPRESSOR OPERATION & MANAGEMENT

run by

NORTHUMBRIA POLICE

BSAC considers that this training achieves
the same objectives as the BSAC Skill
Development Course in

COMPRESSOR OPERATION & MANAGEMENT

and will accept it accordingly

Robin Eccles

Verified

27.8.92

Date

Robin Eccles

Verified by

MARINE RADIO OPERATION

DEVELOPMENT COURSES

ALTERNATIVE TRAINING

M W MOULTON

has completed a course in

BOAT HANDLING

run by

DEPARTMENT OF TRANSPORT

BSAC considers that this training achieves
the same objectives as the BSAC Skill
Development Course in

BOAT HANDLING

and will accept it accordingly

Robin Eccles

Verified

28.8.92

Date

UNDERWATER ENGINEERING

INSTRUCTOR ...Gash...Gillimore... COURSE Hydraul WEEK .... Divers

DAILY DIVING RECORD

NAME	SEPTEMBER								TOTAL
	13	14							
R. SMITH	60	80							
M. MOULTON	67	46							
2. AHAS	47	49							
C. ALWASH	59	64							
SUBJECT									

Divers above attended the Royal Navy Underwater Engineering school and are competent to use the following tool:- Hydraulic Metal Grinder, Stone Grinder, Masonry Drill, Harcawl Chopping, Chain Saw, Impact wrench, Karpy Cable & Sachus Cutter.

C.S. Gillimore
CPO MEM(M)

14 SEP 1990
HORSEA ISLAND

In all cases where decompression sickness is suspected, the
nearest recompression chamber should be contacted. A list
of chambers which may be available in an emergency is
maintained at HMS Vernon, Portsmouth, where expert
advice is also available. Ring 0705-818888 and ask for Duty
Diving Medical Specialist or Duty Lt-Cdr at HMS Vernon.

EVIDENCE OF CURRENT BSAC MEMBERSHIP

Renewal Month

MEMBER TO AFFIX CURRENT

MEMBERSHIP RECEIPT ON THIS PAGE.

FOLD SO THAT IT IS

ENCLOSED WITHIN THIS BOOK.

REPLACE WITH NEW RECEIPT

EACH YEAR.

Apart from the death of diving colleagues, I can say without any doubt I enjoyed every minute of my diving career, both commercially and pleasure.

I spent many happy hours in my leisure time diving all over the world with my wife Kay, having met her at a diving club in Sidcup, Kent, UK, where I enjoyed teaching others the skill of diving.

I always impressed on my students it is the most wonderful thing in the world to be able to submerged yourself underwater and enjoy a world that at one time was inaccessible to the normal man and woman in the street, but to always remember it is an alien environment, that we are only able to share because we have developed equipment that we rely on to breath underwater and to always be mindful and aware that things can go wrong.

Before going in the water check and double check your equipment is fit for purpose, and then when under the water check again. Do not take unnecessary chances, stay with your buddy, and surface with enough air left in your tank for emergencies.

As well as being an author I am also an artist and have painted many underwater scenes taken from various dive locations around the world.

The paintings can be seen and prints purchased at www.mackenzie-moulton.pixels.com click on galleries and you will see one listed as Underwater Paintings.

I have also written two other books about diving, one fictional called 'William Mackenzie a New Beginning' and 'The Metropolitan Police Underwater Search Unit 1983 to 1996'

Now 70 years old I miss my diving but have very happy memories that you can share in this and other books, I even wrote a poem about my diving and will end this book with this, a true event in my basic commercial diving course at The National Police Diving School, Northumbria, UK

The Diving Exercise

It was only a diving exercise
And nothing should be a great surprise.
The task was to lift a great big safe.
And for a police diver this was commonplace.

Other divers had gone before
And whispered what I had in store.
To inflate a bag and raise the safe
Just take your time its not a race.

My turn had come and in I went
Under the water my suit I'd vent.
Descending into the murky depths
The darkness made me breath quite hard.

I found the safe but could not see
But had to release the strap attached
To get the inflation bag free.
I pulled and pulled but it was tight
Unknown to me the safe in flight.

I could not see my predicament
As the safe fell on my arm.
Now I was trapped and in alarm.
It was dark and I was alone
I visualised my own gravestone

I pulled and pushed but all in vain
I tried to lift the safe it was a strain
I got my knife, and dug so hard
Was this it, had god marked my card?

I tried once more using my feet
Against the safe to lever it off my arm
Slowly I managed to free myself
Praying the surface I would meet

I now could see the light above
Did I have enough air left to breath?
would I come out alive
I prayed to be reunited with my love.

The surface came I had no air
I pulled my mask off in despair.
I was alive, I gulped fresh air
I could see the sun how bright and fair

My colleagues cheered and pulled me out
Thank god your safe they all did shout
No more diving for today
You need a drink to take the stress away.

Well that was one of many training dives
And fortunately I have survived.
Not so for many diving friends
Who got the bends and later died.

After joining the Metropolitan Police Underwater Search Unit I had to attend a six week basic commercial diving course with added instruction for preservation of evidence underwater and recovery of bodies,

A poem from my book 'Poems in my life'

I wish you all happy and safe diving
both now and in the future

Mackenzie William Moulton

Author, Artist, Musician, sailor

TO BE CONTINUED
IN
POLICE DIVERS LOG BOOK 2